Daniel Arbuckle's Mas Python

Build powerful Python applications

Daniel Arbuckle

BIRMINGHAM - MUMBAI

Daniel Arbuckle's Mastering Python

First published: June 2017

Production reference: 1300617

Published by Packt Publishing Ltd.
Livery Place
35 Livery Street
Birmingham
B3 2PB, UK.

ISBN 978-1-78728-369-5

Credits

Author
Daniel Arbuckle

Acquisition Editor
Ben Renow-Clarke

Content Development Editor
Monika Sangwan

Technical Editor
Devesh Chugh

Graphics
Kirk D'Penha

Copy Editor
Tom Jacob

Project Coordinator
Suzanne Coutinho

Proofreader
Safis Editing

Indexer
Aishwarya Gangawane

Production Coordinator
Arvindkumar Gupta

About the Author

Daniel Arbuckle gained his PhD in Computer Science from the University of Southern California. He has published numerous papers along with several books and video courses, and he is both a teacher of computer science and a professional programmer.

www.PacktPub.com

For support files and downloads related to your book, please visit www.PacktPub.com. Did you know that Packt offers eBook versions of every book published, with PDF and ePub files available? You can upgrade to the eBook version at www.PacktPub.comand as a print book customer, you are entitled to a discount on the eBook copy. Get in touch with us at service@packtpub.com for more details. At www.PacktPub.com, you can also read a collection of free technical articles, sign up for a range of free newsletters and receive exclusive discounts and offers on Packt books and eBooks.

https://www.packtpub.com/mapt

Get the most in-demand software skills with Mapt. Mapt gives you full access to all Packt books and video courses, as well as industry-leading tools to help you plan your personal development and advance your career.

Why subscribe?

- Fully searchable across every book published by Packt
- Copy and paste, print, and bookmark content
- On demand and accessible via a web browser

Customer Feedback

Thanks for purchasing this Packt book. At Packt, quality is at the heart of our editorial process. To help us improve, please leave us an honest review on this book's Amazon page at www.amazon.com/dp/1787283690.

If you'd like to join our team of regular reviewers, you can email us at customerreviews@packtpub.com. We award our regular reviewers with free eBooks and videos in exchange for their valuable feedback. Help us be relentless in improving our products!

Table of Contents

Preface

Welcome to *Daniel Arbuckle's Mastering Python*. Python is a member of the C family of languages, such as C++ and Java; however, Python is more of a distant cousin, as the designers of Python are quite happy to do things in a different way if it seems better. Therefore, if you're familiar with C or one of its descendant languages, you'll find Python relatively familiar.

The goal of this book is to help you move from being a Python newcomer to being able to use an assortment of advanced techniques. Along with C, C++, and Java, Python is one of the languages that everybody needs to know well. Python is, in my humble opinion, the best all-round language available and it's a whole lot of fun too!

We will progress roughly from entry-level to an advanced level, but for the most part, each chapter is independent of the others. Feel free to skip around to the things that you need to learn, or work through the course in order to get up to speed. So, let's get you there.

What this book covers

Chapter 1, *Python Primer*, is a quick primer on the Python language's syntax and semantics.

Chapter 2, *Setting Up*, is about getting the Python runtime installed and usable.

Chapter 3, *Making a Package*, shows how to create a Python source code package.

Chapter 4, *Basic Best Practices*, covers several of the best practices, including source code formatting rules and the use of tools such as version control in virtual environments.

Chapter 5, *Making a Command-Line Utility*, explains how to create a complete text-mode utility program.

Chapter 6, *Parallel Processing*, shows how to improve the performance of CPU-bound programs in parallel processing.

Chapter 7, *Coroutines and Asynchronous I/O*, explains how to improve the performance of I/O bound programs using asynchronous I/O.

Chapter 8, *Metaprogramming*, covers several different ways in which Python syntax or semantics can be controlled programmatically from within our own source code.

Chapter 9, *Unit Testing*, talks about automated unit testing and test-driven development.

Chapter 10, *Reactive Programming*, is about reactive programming and the RxPY framework.

Chapter 11, *Microservices*, is about creating microservices.

Chapter 12, *Extension Modules and Compiled Code*, talks about linking Python code with system-level code written in C.

What you need for this book

You will need Ubuntu 16.04 and Python (version 3.6). You can also run the code examples on Windows and macOS.

You may opt to use VirtualBox as well to test the code in the book.

Who this book is for

If you are a programmer and are familiar with the basics of Python and you want to broaden your knowledge base to develop projects better and faster, this book is for you. Even if you are not familiar with Python, our book starts with the basics and takes you on a journey to become an expert in the technology.

Conventions

In this book, you will find a number of text styles that distinguish between different kinds of information. Here are some examples of these styles and an explanation of their meaning. Code words in text, database table names, folder names, filenames, file extensions, pathnames, dummy URLs, user input, and Twitter handles are shown as follows: "Using a name variable to look up the stored value is an expression; so is running a function."

A block of code is set as follows:

```
def example_function(name, radius):
    area = math.pi * radius ** 2
    return "The area of {} is {}" .format(name, area)
```

When we wish to draw your attention to a particular part of a code block, the relevant lines or items are set in bold:

```
def example_function(name, radius):
    area = math.pi * radius ** 2
    return "The area of {} is {}" .format(name, area)
```

Any command-line input or output is written as follows:

```
python3 example_1_2_3.py
```

New terms and **important words** are shown in bold. Words that you see on the screen, for example, in menus or dialog boxes, appear in the text like this: "Click on **Environments Variables....**"

Warnings or important notes appear in a box like this.

Tips and tricks appear like this.

Reader feedback

Feedback from our readers is always welcome. Let us know what you think about this book-what you liked or disliked. Reader feedback is important for us as it helps us develop titles that you will really get the most out of. To send us general feedback, simply email feedback@packtpub.com, and mention the book's title in the subject of your message. If there is a topic that you have expertise in and you are interested in either writing or contributing to a book, see our author guide at www.packtpub.com/authors.

Customer support

Now that you are the proud owner of a Packt book, we have a number of things to help you to get the most from your purchase.

Downloading the example code

You can download the example code files for this book from your account at http://www.p acktpub.com. If you purchased this book elsewhere, you can visit http://www.packtpub.c om/support and register to have the files emailed directly to you. You can download the code files by following these steps:

1. Log in or register to our website using your email address and password.
2. Hover the mouse pointer on the **SUPPORT** tab at the top.
3. Click on **Code Downloads & Errata**.
4. Enter the name of the book in the **Search** box.
5. Select the book for which you're looking to download the code files.
6. Choose from the drop-down menu where you purchased this book from.
7. Click on **Code Download**.

Once the file is downloaded, please make sure that you unzip or extract the folder using the latest version of:

- WinRAR / 7-Zip for Windows
- Zipeg / iZip / UnRarX for Mac
- 7-Zip / PeaZip for Linux

The code bundle for the book is also hosted on GitHub at https://github.com/PacktPubl ishing/Daniel-Arbuckles-Mastering-Python. We also have other code bundles from our rich catalog of books and videos available at https://github.com/PacktPublishing/. Check them out!

Errata

Although we have taken every care to ensure the accuracy of our content, mistakes do happen. If you find a mistake in one of our books-maybe a mistake in the text or the code-we would be grateful if you could report this to us. By doing so, you can save other readers from frustration and help us improve subsequent versions of this book. If you find any errata, please report them by visiting http://www.packtpub.com/submit-errata, selecting your book, clicking on the **Errata Submission Form** link, and entering the details of your errata. Once your errata are verified, your submission will be accepted and the errata will be uploaded to our website or added to any list of existing errata under the Errata section of that title. To view the previously submitted errata, go to https://www.packtpub.com/books/content/support and enter the name of the book in the search field. The required information will appear under the **Errata** section.

Piracy

Piracy of copyrighted material on the Internet is an ongoing problem across all media. At Packt, we take the protection of our copyright and licenses very seriously. If you come across any illegal copies of our works in any form on the Internet, please provide us with the location address or website name immediately so that we can pursue a remedy. Please contact us at copyright@packtpub.com with a link to the suspected pirated material. We appreciate your help in protecting our authors and our ability to bring you valuable content.

Questions

If you have a problem with any aspect of this book, you can contact us at questions@packtpub.com, and we will do our best to address the problem.

1
Python Primer

In this chapter, we will be covering the basic syntax of Python, its built-in data structures, functions, classes, its standard library, and the new features in the latest versions of Python. If you need to get up to speed on the language, this is where we'll do that. We'll walk through, step by step, covering the following topics:

- Python basic syntax and block structure
- Built-in data structures and comprehensions
- First-class functions and classes
- Extensive standard library
- What's new in Python

Python basic syntax and block structure

This section primarily provides a basic understanding of the Python language constructs. If you feel you already have a solid grasp of Python, feel free to skip ahead.

Let's get down to the nuts and bolts.

A Python program is written as source code in one or more .py files and consists of statements and expressions as shown in the following screenshot:

```
print(1)
print(1 + 1)
print(3 * 1 + 2)
print(3 * (1 + 2))

if 2 > 1:
    print("One is the loneliest number")
else:
    print('Two is the lonliest number?')
```

Both statements and expressions tell Python to do something. The difference is that expressions can be combined to form more complex expressions, while statements can be combined with expressions, but not with other statements.

For example, a statement looks like this:

```
if 2 > 1:
```

An expression looks like this:

```
print ("One is the loneliest number")
```

Python source code files are executed from top to bottom as soon as they're loaded by the Python runtime. This means that for simple programs, we could just write a series of statements in a .py file and then tell Python to run them. In the preceding example, the if and else parts are statements or a single statement with two parts, if you prefer to think of it that way. Everything else is an expression. For more complex programs, we need a more structured approach.

Like most programming languages, Python lets us create functions and classes in order to organize our code.

If you don't know what functions or classes are, you could think of functions as miniature programs that can be used as building blocks for larger programs and classes as combinations of functions and data to create new kinds of data.

Basic building blocks

To organize our code, we can divide it into four basic building blocks. We'll discuss each of these separately for understanding their role and importance in the Python code. These are as follows:

- Functions
- Variables
- Expressions
- Classes

Functions

We'll start with a brief look at functions. Functions are created using a def statement, which is a statement using the def keyword as its identifying component. As I said earlier, Python executes the statements in a .py file, starting from the top, as shown in the following screenshot:

```python
import math

def example_function(name, radius):
    area = math.pi * radius ** 2
    return "The area of {} is {}".format(name, area)

print(example_function('Bob', 5))
```

When Python executes a def statement, it creates a function as a result. This means that the code that runs before the def statement does not see the function because it doesn't exist yet. The part of the def line inside parentheses is called the **parameter list**:

```python
example_function(name, radius):
```

The parameter list is a list of internal names for data values that are given to the function as the input. Outside the function, these values might have different names or no names at all, but inside, they'll be stored in these variables.

The indented block of code immediately after the def line is called the **function body**, and you could think of it as the source code of the function:

```
def example_function(name, radius):
    area = math.pi * radius ** 2
    return "The area of {} is {}" .format(name, area)
```

The following screenshot shows the output of the preceding example:

```
devesh@devesh-VirtualBox:~$ python3 example_1_2_3.py
The area of Bob is 78.53981633974483
```

The code inside the function body is an exception to the rule about running Python code from the top to the bottom of the file. This code is stored away and then executed later, when we tell the function to run.

> Like the code in a file, the code in a function runs from top to bottom, one statement or expression at a time.

If you're more familiar with C++ or Java, you may be wondering where the function *parameter types* and *return types* are. In Python, the data type is inherent in each data value, so the runtime always knows what type of data we're working with and whether what we're trying to do is a valid operation for that data type. Thus, for the most part, we don't need explicit data types.

Python programmers sometimes talk about *duck typing*, which is a reference to the following saying:

If it quacks like a duck, it's probably a duck.

What they mean by this saying is that if the operations we're trying to perform on a data value work, it doesn't really matter if it's precisely the kind of data we expected. It's probably close enough. If they don't work, Python will tell us what went wrong and where, which is often more useful to know than the kind of information that can be determined by comparing data types alone.

> For situations where we want or need to specify data types, we can use function annotations and the standard library typing module.

Function decorators, which we'll discuss in later chapters, can provide a convenient way of enforcing these annotations.

Variables

The second major building block of a Python program is called a **variable**. A variable is pretty much just a box for storing a data value. The variable has a name and we can use that name to access the data stored in the variable or to replace the data with a new value.

The function parameters in the previous examples were variables, as was `area`:

```
(name, radius):
```

To set the data stored in a variable, we use an *assignment* statement. An assignment is a statement, so remember this means that it can't be combined with any other statement. It gets a line of source code all for itself and the expressions that are part of it.

An assignment statement consists of the variable's name on the left-hand side of an equal to symbol and the value we want to store in the variable on the right-hand side, as shown in the following code:

```
outer = "Hello world"
```

If the variable didn't already exist, it will be created. Irrespective of whether the variable existed before or not, the value is stored in the variable.

Variables that are created inside a function are only visible inside that function and each time the function runs they're created a new.

The following code provides an example of this in action:

```
outer = "Hello world"
def example_function(param):
    inner = "Hello function: {}".format(param)
    print(inner, outer)
example_function("first")
example_function("second")
print(inner)
```

The last line of the preceding example demonstrates that the variable created inside the function does not exist for code outside the function, as shown in the following output of the code:

```
devesh@devesh-VirtualBox:~$ python3 example_1_2_4.py
Hello function: First Hello world
Hello function: Second Hello world
Traceback (most recent call last):
  File "example_1_2_4.py", line 9, in <module>
    print(inner)
NameError: name 'inner' is not defined
```

This code example also shows what happens when we try to ask Python to do something impossible. It tells us what we did wrong and gives us the information about where the problem occurred and how we got there.

Expressions

The third major building block of Python programs is **expressions**. We've seen expressions in every example so far because it's nearly impossible to do anything in Python without using expressions.

Expressions consist of data values and operations to perform on those data values. The very simple expressions are a single data value and with no operations, for example, a single number. More complex expressions involve at least one operation and probably more data values as well, for example, adding two numbers or calculating the area, as shown in the following code example:

```python
import math

def example_function(name: str, radius: float) -> str:
  area = math.pi * radius ** 2
  return "The area of {} is {}" .format(name, area)

print(example_function('Bob', 5))
```

All expressions produce a resulting data value of some sort; for example, adding two numbers produces the sum as another number, while concatenating two text strings produces the concatenation as another text string. Using a `name` variable to look up the stored value is an expression, so is running a function.

> If the function doesn't explicitly return a value, the result is a special value called **none**.

Anywhere we need a value, we can use any expression that produces the needed value. It doesn't matter whether the expression is a simple number, such as 55, a variable name, a complex combination of values and operators, a function call, or any other expression. At least, it doesn't matter as far as the final result is concerned. Some expressions take less time to execute than others, so speed can be a factor.

Classes

The final fundamental building block we're going to discuss in this section is **classes**. The word class is a synonym for category or type; in this case, it is referring to data values.

A class defines a new kind of data value by describing a set of internal data and operations for that type of data value. This is done primarily by defining a group of functions that make up the class. A special function called __init__ is used to set up the internal data for a new data value of this type, and the rest of the functions define the operations on an existing data value of this type:

```
class Frood:
    def __init__(self, age):
        self.age = age
        print("Frood initialized")

    def anniversary(self):
        self.age += 1
        print("Frood is now {} years old".format(self.age))

f1 = Frood(12)
f2 = Frood(97)
f1.anniversary()
f2.anniversary()
f1.anniversary()
f2.anniversary()
```

All the functions of a class receive a parameter called self, as shown in the preceding code example for classes. This parameter is the data value being operated on. That's different from C++ or Java because while those languages do basically the same thing, the parameter is implicit instead of being an explicit part of the function's parameter list.

Class functions, including __init__, should store and retrieve data from self when they want to manipulate the data value that they're connected to.

Classes support **inheritance** and **multiple inheritance**, but we won't go into that in detail at this point in the book.

In the preceding example, we created a new data type called `Frood` and then made two separate data values of that type. Then, we used the `anniversary` function that we created as part of the class to modify each of them.

The output of the code example for classes is as follows:

```
devesh@devesh-VirtualBox:~$ python3 example_1_2_5.py
Frood initialized
Frood initialized
Frood is now 13 years old
Frood is now 98 years old
Frood is now 14 years old
Frood is now 99 years old
```

The two instances maintain their internal variables with different values, as shown in the preceding output.

Flow control statements

Python has several flow control statements that will be familiar to people who know another language in the C family. For example, Python has loops and `if`, `elif`, and `else` branches (shown in the following code example):

```python
selector = 5

if selector < 3:
    print("less than three")
elif selector < 6:
    print("less than six")
else:
    print("six or more")
while selector > 0"
    print('selector is {}' .format(selector))
    selector -=1

for x in ['a', 'b', 'c', 'd']:
    print(x)
```

```
for x in range(5):
    print(x)
```

Python also has a `for` loop statement, but it's not like the `for` loops in C, C++, or Java. Instead of counting through numbers, the `for` loop iterates through the values. If we actually want to count through numbers with a `for` loop, that's easily done using a `range` iterator, as shown in the following screenshot in the output of the preceding code example:

```
devesh@devesh-VirtualBox:~$ python3 example_1_2_6.py
less than six
selector is 5
selector is 4
selector is 3
selector is 2
selector is 1
a
b
c
d
0
1
2
3
4
```

Before we wrap-up this section, there's one last thing I should comment on and that's Python's views on **indentation** to signify the block structure.

Indentation

Most other programming languages have explicit symbols that indicate the beginning of a block and the end of a block. However, it's a common practice in all of those languages to indent blocks so that humans find the code easier to read. In fact, failure to do so is often taken as a sign that a programmer is an amateur. This means that the block structure in most languages is actually represented in two different ways: the symbols and the indentation. By incorporating indentation into syntax without the need for explicit symbols, Python both removes this duplication and ensures that the code is readable.

With that, we've come to the end of this section. In the next section, we'll look at some of Python's built-in data structures and the data processing syntax.

Python's built-in data structures and comprehensions

Now, let's take a look at the core data structure types of Python. These aren't the only data structures available, of course, because it's fairly easy to create data structures using classes. However, these data structures are built right into the heart of Python and they're highly efficient, so it's a good idea to be very familiar with them.

The first thing to understand is that data structures are themselves data values similar to a filing cabinet-they're one thing that contains many things. Like any other data value, they can be stored in a variable or used as part of an expression.

Dictionaries

The first data structure we're going to look at is Python's dictionary. A dictionary consists of any number of key-value pairs. The key can be used to get or set the value or remove the pair from the dictionary entirely.

Similar data structures in other languages are sometimes called maps or hash tables.

There are several ways to create a dictionary in Python. The simplest is to use a dictionary expression, which is just a pair of curly brackets surrounding the key-value pairs we want in the dictionary. Each key-value pair is marked with a colon between the key and value, and each pair is separated by a comma, as shown in the following code example:

```
example_dict = {'a' :1, 'b' :2, 'c' :3}
```

When this expression runs, the result is a dictionary object containing the keys and their values. We can also use the `dict` class to create dictionary objects:

```
another_dict = dict()
```

If we don't want to use the special syntax to access one of the stored values in a dictionary, we use a lookup expression. This means that we place square brackets containing the key we want to look up after an expression that gives us the dictionary. Usually, this means, the name of the variable containing the dictionary, an open square bracket, a sub-expression that gives us the key, and then a closing square bracket:

```
example_dict['b']
2
```

We can also use the `dict.get` function if we prefer not to use the special syntax:

```
example_dict.get('c')
3
```

List

The next data type we're going to look at is a **list**, which can be created with the list expression. A list expression is just a pair of square brackets surrounding the data values we want to store in the list, with each value separated by a comma. It is not necessary that each of the values be of the same type. The code example for a list is as follows:

```
>>> example_list = ['a', 'b', 'c', 'd', 'e', 'f']
>>> another_list = list()
>>> example_list[-1]
'f'
>>> example_list[0]
'a'
>>> example_list[1]
'b'
>>> example_list[-2]
'e'
```

In the preceding example, they're strings, but they could be numbers, or a list, or any other kind of data mixed together. We can use a lookup expression to retrieve data values.

Unlike with a dictionary though, the keys for a list are integers. That's because instead of associating key values with data values, a list just stores its data values in order. The key for the very first item in the list is 0. The key for the next item is 1, and so on. We can also use negative integers for the key. We still get a data value out, but it's counted from the end of the list instead of the beginning, with the item at −1 being the last item in the list.

We can use the `list.append` function to add a new item at the end of the list or its `insert` function to add a new item anywhere as shown in the following code:

```
>>> example_list.append('happy')
>>> example_list[-1]
'happy'
```

The list will automatically grow to be large enough to hold all of the data we put into it.

Tuple

The next data structure we'll look at is the **tuple**. A tuple expression is any sequence of value expressions separated by commas if it happens in the place where the language wasn't already expecting to see a comma.

However, it's common and smart to put parentheses around most tuple expressions because it avoids ambiguity. The code example for tuple is as follows:

```
>>> example_tuple = ('Hello', 12, None)
>>> another_tuple = tuple([1, 2, 3, 'jump'])
>>> example_tuple[1]
12
```

Like a list, data values can be retrieved from a tuple using numbers. However, we can't add more data to a tuple, and we cannot replace one data value with another.

Why would we want a data structure like that?

Well, there are several reasons. We can list them as follows:

- First, because they are constant, tuples make good dictionary keys or set members, but we'll get to that in a while.
- Second, they fill a different conceptual role than lists. We tend to expect every member of a list to be the same type, such as a list of names or a list of ages. Lists are sort of like columns of a database in that way. We tend to expect tuples to contain different types of data in each element, but we expect them to be related to each other, such as a name in the first element and an age in the second. To continue our analogy, tuples are something like rows in a database.
- Third, tuples tend to be slightly more efficient for the computer to work with, both in terms of time and memory usage. So, in optimization situations, they are preferable to lists when they are sufficient for the task.

Set

The final data structure we'll look at is the **set**. A set is a collection of data values without keys; like a list, but in no particular order, like a dictionary. We can create a set using a set expression, which is a pair of curly brackets around comma-separated values, as shown in the following code example:

```
>>> example_set = {'a', 'b', 'c', 'd', 'e', 'f'}
>>> another_set = set()
>>> 'b' in example_set
True
>>> 'b' in another_set
False
```

Locating a specific value in a set is fast, as is adding or removing a value, as shown in the following example:

```
>>> example_set.add('b')
>>> print(example_set)
{'e', 'c', 'f', 'd', 'a', 'b'}
>>> example_set.discard('b')
>>> 'b' in example_set
False
```

Each value can only be in the set once. Sets support a bunch of mathematical operations, such as union and intersection, and are generally more useful than might be obvious at first, though we can't really prove that here in this section.

Comprehension

Python has a special kind of expression called a **comprehension**. Comprehensions are variations of the special syntax for creating dictionaries, lists, and sets.

Let's look at some examples. Here we see a list comprehension:

```python
capitals = [x.upper() for x in example_list]
```

What this expression does is that it creates a new list containing the uppercase versions of the words in the old list.

The first part after the opening square bracket is an `x.upper()` expression. This expression describes how to derive a member of the new list from a member of the old list. After that is the `for` keyword, then the name of the `x` variable we used in the first expression to represent the values from the old list. Then, the keyword is followed by the `example_list` expression that gives us the old list and the closing square bracket. The code output is as follows:

```python
>>> capitals = [x.upper() for x in example_list]
>>> print(capitals)
['E', 'A', 'D', 'F', 'B', 'C']
```

The dictionary and set comprehensions are very similar. If we want to use both the key and the value of an existing dictionary in a comprehension, we need to use the `dict.items` function, and dictionary comprehensions need to specify both the key and value separated by a colon, as shown in this example:

```python
squares = {k: v ** 2 for k, v in example_dict.items()}
```

As shown in the following screenshot, notice that the resulting data type depends on what sort of comprehension we used, not on what sort of data structure we used as the source of data:

```
>>> squares = {k: v ** 2 for k, v in example_dict.items()}
>>> print(squares)
{'c': 9, 'b': 4, 'a': 1}
>>> codes = {ord(x) for x in example_set}
>>> print(codes)
{97, 98, 99, 100, 101, 102}
>>> capital_keys = {x.upper() for x in example_dict.keys()}
>>> print(capital_keys)
{'A', 'B', 'C'}
>>> type(capital_keys)
<class 'set'>
```

We can use a list comprehension to create a list of data pulled from the values of a dictionary, for example, or, as we did here, we can use the set comprehension to create a set.

Tuples are slightly different, but only slightly. A tuple comprehension would look exactly like a different syntactic element called a **generator expression**. The code example for tuple comprehension is as follows:

```
>>> example_tuple = ('Hello', 12, None)
>>> stringified = tuple(str(x) for x in example_tuple)
>>> print(stringified)
('Hello', '12', 'None')
```

Python's designers hate ambiguity; so instead, if we want the equivalent of a tuple comprehension, we pass a generator expression to a tuple constructor.

That's it for this quick introduction to Python's built-in data structures. In the next section, we're going to look at some useful, but possibly surprising, traits of functions and classes that are significantly different from C, C++, or Java.

First-class functions and classes

In Python, functions and classes are first-class objects. The phrase **first-class object** is a fancy way of saying that the data values can be accessed, modified, stored, and otherwise manipulated by the program they are a part of. In Python, a function is just as much a data value as a text string is. The same goes for classes.

When a function definition statement is executed, it stores the resulting function in a variable with the name that was specified in the `def` statement, as shown in the following screenshot:

```
>>> def foo():
...     pass
...
>>> foo
<function foo at 0x7f68ccadb9d8>
```

This variable isn't special; it's just like any other variable holding the value. This means that we can use it in expressions, assign the value to other values, or even store a different value in place of the original function.

The function value itself contains quite a few attribute variables, which we can access. More usefully, most of the time, we can add attributes to a `function` object, allowing us to store custom information about a function as part of the function and access that information later, as shown in the following code example:

```
>>> bar = foo
>>> bar
<function foo at 0x7f68ccadb9d8>
>>> foo = 5
>>> foo
5
>>> bar
<function foo at 0x7f68ccadb9d8>
>>> bar.__name__
'foo'
```

One common task that first-class functions make easy is assigning handlers to events. To bind the **handler** function to an event in Python, we just pass the `function` object as a parameter when we call the **binding** function, as shown here:

```
>>> import atexit
>>> atexit.register(bar)
<function foo at 0x7f68ccadb9d8>
```

That's a significant improvement over the hoops that C++ or Java imposes on us to do something similar. As function definition statements, class definition statements create a class object and store it in a variable. This can be confusing at first. Classes describe the type of object, how can they be objects themselves?

Think of it this way-a blueprint for a house describes the type of building, but the blueprint is still a thing in its own, right? It's the same with class objects. This means that like function objects, class objects can be stored in variables, and otherwise, be treated as data values. Most interestingly, they could be used as parameters to function calls.

The defaultdict class

As an example of why that's interesting, consider this-Python's standard library contains a data structure class called defaultdict, which is like a dictionary except, when we try to look up a key that isn't already in the dictionary. It creates a new value and adds it to the dictionary, before returning it to the code that tried the lookup, as shown here:

```
>>> import collections
>>> d = collections.defaultdict(list)
>>> d['not in here']
[]
```

How does the defaultdict class know how to create the default value?

The defaultdict class knows because we gave it class as a parameter when we created the defaultdict class. Thus, if we want a dictionary of list, we can give the defaultdict class the list class, as its *how to make a default* parameter. As an aside, defaultdict can also work with a function, as its *how to make a default* parameter.

The defaultdict class actually doesn't care what that parameter is, as long as the object we passed can create a new object whenever the defaultdict class needs a new default. This is an example of the duck typing we mentioned in the previous section. It doesn't matter whether the parameter is a function, a class, or anything else, so long as it behaves properly. If it doesn't behave properly, we'll be told what went wrong and where.

Attributes

We discussed a little while ago that we could add attributes to function objects, which is often handy. We could do something similar with classes, with one big difference- attributes that we add to functions are only visible to the code that has access to that function object, which usually doesn't include the code of the function itself, but attributes that we add to class objects are visible to any code that has access to the class object or to an object of the type described by the class.

This means that if we add an attribute to a class, the functions defined in that class will be able to access that attribute through the `self` parameter, as shown in the following code example:

```
>>> class Example:
...     class_trait = 5
...     def __init__(self):
...         self.instance_trait = 7
...
>>> Example
<class '__main__.Example'>
>>> def new_function(self):
...     print(self.instance_trait, self.class_trait)
...
>>> Example.added = new_function
>>> x = Example()
>>> x.added()
7 5
>>> Example.class_trait = 9
>>> x.added()
7 9
```

We need to be careful when adding attributes to classes because if we accidentally overwrite one of the class' attributes, we could break the class.

We have a greater ability to manipulate classes than functions. So, we need to use that ability more thoughtfully. Also, notice that, in this example, one of the attributes we added to the class is a function, which then proceeded to work exactly as if it had been defined as a part of the class from the beginning.

Next, let's take a short tour of some of the highlights of Python's standard library.

The standard library

The library of code that comes pre-installed with Python is extensive, so we're not going into the details. The goal here is to come away with an understanding of the breadth of quality tools we have available, so if we need them in the future then we know where to look. Thus, we're going to just briefly touch on many useful things. You can find the official documentation on the standard library at
`https://docs.python.org/3/library/index.html`.

Different types of packages

The index page contains a list of the different packages available to you in Python's standard library. Let's briefly run through them in order.

First of all, there is the `Collections` package, which contains even more data structures: `https://docs.python.org/3/library/collections.html`.

The `Collections` package contains the `defaultdict` class that we spoke about in the previous section. The `Collections` package also contains an `OrderedDict` parameter that remembers the order in which the items were inserted and gives them back in the same order when we iterate over it. A `deque` class is a variation on tuples that uses names to access the element and a `PseudoDict` parameter that provides a composite view of several other dictionaries.

There are a few other data structures in there as well. One common data structure missing from the collections package is a `PriorityQueue` parameter, but that's just because it has its own package called `heapq`:

`https://docs.python.org/3/library/heapq.html`

Python's `PriorityQueue` operations are implemented as functions that work with built-in lists to add and remove items according to the **heap** property.

Storing and retrieving data is an extremely common need for programs and the `pickle` package makes it easy:

`https://docs.python.org/3/library/pickle.html`

Inside the `pickle` package are classes and functions that facilitate transforming arbitrary Python data into a sequence of bytes that can be stored in a file, sent across the network, or whatever you need. The `pickle` package also has the tools to reverse the process and transform those bytes back into fully-fledged Python data objects.

Also, in the vein of storing data, the `sqlite3` package provides complete access to the SQLite database manager, allowing us to take advantage of a complete transactional relational database:

https://docs.python.org/3/library/sqlite.html

Third-party packages to access other database systems follow pretty much the same interface, so it's easy to make the switch to a different database later, if needed.

The `json` package is also relevant to data handling. It parses or generates the de facto standard **Internet Data Exchange (IDX)** format:

https://docs.python.org/3/library/json.html

The `json` package is smart, so it handles **JSON (JavaScript Object Notation)** objects, arrays, strings, numbers, null values, and so on, in a sensible way.

Mapping them onto the proper Python datatypes, the `base64` package encodes bytes into base64, or decodes base64 into bytes:

https://docs.python.org/3/library/base64.html

There are several other similar packages for `binhex`, `uu` code, and so on, as well.

The `html` and `xml` packages provide all sorts of utilities for dealing with the major internet markup languages, including parsers and the document object model:

https://docs.python.org/3/library/html.html

The `urllib` package provides us with convenient ways to retrieve data from URLs or to send data to them:

https://docs.python.org/3/library/urllib.html

In particular, the `urllib.request.url` open function is extremely useful.

The `itertools` and `functools` packages provide an assortment of utilities having to do with functional programming paradigms:

https://docs.python.org/3/library/itertools.html

In particular, the `functools` package allows for us to create partially applied functions and the `itertools` package lets us concatenate iterators.

The `enum` package contains support for creating and using named enumerations:

`https://docs.python.org/3/library/enum.html`

Each enumeration is a distinct data type, like a class.

The `pathlib` package contains classes and functions that provide a cross-platform abstraction of file and file path operations:

`https://docs.python.org/3/library/pathlib.html`

The `inspect` package is interesting and quite useful. It provides us with functions that can be used to gather information about data objects, particularly about functions and classes. If we want to know the names of functions, parameters, or we want to access an object's documentation, or any number of things along those lines, the `inspect` package will get us there:

`https://docs.python.org/3/library/inspect.html`

The packages we just looked at are by no means the complete list of what's available in the standard library, but hopefully they give some idea of the depth and breadth of what we get just by installing Python. Taking a look through the library documentation on `https://www.python.org/` is highly recommended for people who want to get the most out of Python. There are some particularly useful packages that we didn't mention at all. That's because there are whole other sections devoted to them later in the book.

So, that brings us to the end of our overview of the standard library.

What's new in modern Python

In this section, we're going to take a look at a few of the changes that have occurred in the latest releases of Python, specifically we will look at these:

- The syntactic changes
- The changes in the packages
- Other changes

Let's get started!

The changes in the syntactic

Since version 3.5, Python has three new groups of syntactic editions. The first of these groups is the introduction of keywords for describing **coroutines**. Python already supported coroutines, but the keywords make things clear and sometimes simpler. We'll be discussing coroutines in depth in a later chapter, so we won't go into this any further now.

The second piece of the new syntax is the introduction of the @ symbol as an infix binary operator. This means that placing an @ symbol between two sub-expressions is now a valid Python expression, just like placing a + symbol between the sub-expressions would be as shown in the following screenshot:

```
>>> 5 @ 10
Traceback (most recent call last):
  File "<stdin>", line 1, in <module>
TypeError: unsupported operand type(s) for @: 'int' and 'int'
```

However, since no built-in data type supports the @ symbol operator yet, we won't be finding much use for it in this book. The intended semantic meaning of the @ symbol is that it should represent matrix multiplication and it was added to improve support for an interoperability between third-party packages that implement matrixes and matrix operations.

The third piece of new syntax is an expansion of Python's pre-existing syntax for using lists and dictionaries to provide the parameter values when invoking a function.

Before, it was possible to put an asterisk (*) before a list of values to indicate that those values should be assigned to the parameters in the same order that they appeared in the list. Here is the code example for a single asterisk:

```
>>>
>>> def needs_params(a, b, c):
...         print(a, b, c)
...
>>> values = [1, 2, 3]
>>> needs_params(*values)
1 2 3
```

Similarly, * before two values was used to indicate that the values in a dictionary with text string keys should be assigned to the function's parameters by name, as shown here:

```
>>> partial_values1 = [1, 2]
>>> partial_values2 = [3]
>>> needs_params(*partial_values1, *partial_values2)
1 2 3
>>> needs_params(*partial_values2, *partial_values1)
3 1 2
>>> combined_values = [*partial_values1, *partial_values2]
>>> combined_values
[1, 2, 3]
```

The new syntax is just that we can now use more than one list or dictionary in this way, and that we can use the same asterisk and double asterisk syntax for constructing tuples, lists, dictionaries, and sets.

We mentioned earlier that while Python attaches data types to data values rather than variables, it is possible to use function annotations to describe the expected types of function parameters' return values.

Changes in packages

Python now includes a package called `typing` in the standard library that contains classes and functions supporting the usage of type hints.

Python also includes a package called `zipapp` in the standard library.

For `typing` visit the following website:
https://docs.python.org/3/library/typing.html

For `zipapp`, visit this website:
https://docs.python.org/3/library/zipapp.html

The `zipapp` package makes it easy to construct `.pyz` files. A `.pyz` file is an archive file containing Python code and arbitrary read-only data, which the Python runtime is able to execute as a self-contained program. Once a program is debugged and ready for distribution, packaging it into a `.pyz` file is a simple and smart way to hand it to the users.

Other changes in Python packages

Some low-level improvements have been made in Python since version 3.5, such as faster reading of `filesystem` directories, automatic retrying of interrupted operating system calls, and a `math.isclose` function for checking whether two numbers are approximately equal.

There are also a bunch of more minor additions that improve things throughout the standard library, all backwards compatible with earlier Python 3 versions.

In the rare cases where something is added that breaks backwards compatibility, it's not enabled by default. For such a change, if we want to use it, we'd have to specifically mark our code as supporting the change. Those changes will not become standard until two versions later, so a breaking change in Python 3.5 would not become the default until Python version 3.7, with Python 3.5 and 3.6 issuing warnings when they encounter code that depends on the changing feature.

In Python 3.5, there was only one such change-a small and smart alteration in the iteration protocol. It shouldn't have any effect on code that works properly, but technically it's a change in the interface and so it gets the full wait two versions treatment.

If you want more detail about any of these changes I've mentioned, or if you ever want to find out what's changed between versions of Python, the documentation on `https://docs.python.org/3/` always contains a **what's new** document that goes into some detail about new features and provides links to the full documentation.

> For details on the Python 3.6 what's new document, visit the following link:
> `https://docs.python.org/3/whatsnew/3.6.html`

I always look forward to reading the what's new document for each release of Python, to find out what new toys I've just been handed.

So, we've now taken a high-level view of the Python standard library, introducing us to some of the more useful items it contains. That brings us to the end of our Python primer.

Summary

In this chapter, we looked at some fundamentals of the Python programming language. We have seen how to create and access those data structures, and how to use comprehensions to create and transform data structures based on existing ones.

We looked briefly at what it means for Python to have first-class functions and classes, and how that can affect the possibilities open to us as programmers.

We briefly talked about some of the high points of the Python standard library. We also quickly covered the syntax, basic assumptions, and fundamental tools of the Python programming language.

In the next chapter, we're going to see how to set up a Python programming environment for us to work in for the remainder of the course and learn a bit about how to integrate third-party code.

2
Setting Up

In the previous chapter, we took a brief tour of the Python programming language. In this chapter, we will look at various ways to download and install the correct version of Python, then we will see how to run Python code. In the last couple of sections of this chapter, we'll see how to begin taking advantage of the wide variety of publicly available Python code that can be found on the internet.

The topics covered in this chapter are as follows:

- Downloading and installing Python
- Using the command line and the interactive shell
- Installing packages with `pip`
- Finding packages in the Python package index

Downloading and installing Python

The topic of this section is downloading and installing the Python runtime and standard library. For this, let's first take a look at the download page, `https://www.python.org/`, which is, of course, the authoritative place to find Python. You will learn a little bit about which versions of Python exist and the one we should choose for this book. Then, we'll move on to how to set up Python for this book. Finally, we'll check that everything worked the way we wanted.

Before we can really begin working with Python, we need to make sure we've got the language interpreter and libraries properly installed. The first step for that is to decide which version of the language to install.

Choosing a suitable version

There are currently two common varieties of Python in use. One of them is Python version 2.7, which is the final version of the Python 2 series. The Python community has promised to maintain version 2.7 independently, making it a very stable target for development. The other common version is Python 3, which at the time of writing this book is in version 3.6.

Python 3 is where the Python community is innovating. The releases are always backward compatible with earlier version 3 releases, but new exciting features are added regularly. During the change to version 3, the language in the libraries was changed in subtle ways, as you can see in the comparison of the following two code snippets:

```
from urllib2 import urlopen, URLError

def fetch_email(url):

    try:
        date = urlopen(url).read()
        return data.split('mailto: ')[1].split('"')[0]
    except:
        print error
        return 'invalid@example.com'
```

```
from urllib.request import urlopen
from urllib.error import URLError

def fetch_email(url):
    try:
        data = urlopen(url).read().decode('utf8')
        return data.split('mailto:')[1].split('"')[0]
    except (IndexError, URLError) as error:
        print(error)
        return 'invalid@example.com'
```

In the preceding screenshot, on the left-hand side is Python 2 and on the right-hand side you see an equivalent code in Python 3. They are almost the same, but have differences, such as placement of parentheses, a few keywords, and a slightly different structure than the standard library. You're free to pick whichever version or versions you want for your own projects, but for this book, we'll be using Python version 3.

Now that we have picked the version, let's install it.

Installing Python

If you're a Windows or Mac user, you can download an installer directly from the Python website (https://www.python.org/downloads/). Pick the installer appropriate for your computer, download it, and run it for any platform. We also have the option of downloading the source code, compiling it, and installing Python that way.

Unix and Linux users, as well as Mac users who prefer it, have the option to install Python through their package manager instead. For systems which integrate a package manager, this is probably the best and easiest choice. If we use the package manager, this next part is probably already done, otherwise we need to make sure that the Python programs are able to run from the command line.

On macOS and Unix-like operating systems, all we need is to add a line to the profile or the `bashrc` file in our home directory:

- macOS X (edit ~/.profile):

export   PATH=<pydir>:$PATH

- Unix/Linux (edit ~/.bashrc):

export PATH=<pydir>:$PATH

- Windows:

1. Open **Advanced System Settings** in **Control Panel**.
2. Click on **Environments Variables...**.
3. Edit **PATH**.
4. Add `;<pydir>` at the end.

Windows is only slightly more involved, as you'll need to open up the **Control Panel** and locate the **Environment Variables** screen. In each of the preceding examples, `pydir` is the directory where you installed Python—`C:\python36`, for example.

Once we've got the path environment variable set, we should be good to go. To check that-open a Terminal window (Command Prompt on Windows) and type `Python`, then hit *Enter*. If you don't know how to open the Terminal, don't worry, we'll talk about that in more detail in the next chapter.

Also, if you are a Unix user and you do not receive the correct result, it is potentially because the `bashrc` file or profile has not been executed yet. You may need to log out and log back in again.

 If the Python interactive shell starts up when we type `python` into the Terminal, we're good to go. If it doesn't, go back to double-check the changes that we made to the path environment variable because that's the piece that tells the operating system where to look for programs.

That's it for setting up.

If you're feeling adventurous, you can experiment with the interactive shell that we just started up. Try typing in mathematical expressions and see what happens. In the next section, we'll look more closely at running Python code using the command line and the interactive shell.

Using the command line and the interactive shell

Since, we looked at installing Python, let's try our hand at making Python actually do things using the textual interface.

Text-based user interfaces are very useful to programmers; they provide a quick and easy way to interact with programs while they're in development, experiment with code (which is, after all, text), and access documentation.

Opening a command-line window

How you open a command-line window depends on the operating system you're using.

- On Windows 7, open the Start menu and type CMD into the **Run** box.
- In Windows 8, press the Windows key and then type CMD and select **Command Prompt**.
- On Windows 10, press the Windows key and select **Command Prompt**.
- On macOS, navigate to **Applications** | **Utilities** | **Terminal**.
- On Linux or other Unix-style operating systems, the precise mechanism for opening a command-line window varies, but they all have the ability to do it; look for the words **xterm**, **terminal**, or **shell**.

Python interactive shell

Now that we've got a command-line window, we'll go straight into the Python interactive shell. We do that by typing `python` into the command-line window.

If you have multiple versions of Python installed and we want to interact with a specified version, we can explicitly choose the version from the command line by typing in that version's name. For example, if we type `python3`, we'll explicitly start up some version of Python 3.X:

```
devesh@devesh-VirtualBox:~$ python3
Python 3.5.2 (default, Nov 17 2016, 17:05:23)
[GCC 5.4.0 20160609] on linux
Type "help", "copyright", "credits" or "license" for more information.
```

 The `python3` command is used for Linux users. Windows users should type `python` command line to work.

Now, the fun really starts!

When we see the `>>>` prompt, we can type in any Python expression or statement and see the result immediately (as shown in the following screenshot of code example):

```
>>> 2 + 2
4
>>> x = 7
>>> (x + 5) / 2
6.0
>>> 'lucky' + x
Traceback (most recent call last):
  File "<stdin>", line 1, in <module>
TypeError: Can't convert 'int' object to str implicitly
>>> 'lucky' + str(x)
'lucky7'
```

This is incredibly useful because it means that we don't have to remember every detail about how functions work, what class members are called, which exceptions are raised under what circumstances, and so on. Whenever we're unsure about something, we can just open up an interactive shell and find out. So, let's discuss this using a simple example.

Let's imagine we're working on an application that uses Python's set data type and we're unsure about what exception gets raised. When we try to add a set to itself, we could go digging through the documentation, but it's quicker and easier to just create a set in the interactive shell and try adding it to itself:

```
>>> y = set()
>>> y.add(y)
Traceback (most recent call last):
  File "<stdin>", line 1, in <module>
TypeError: unhashable type: 'set'
```

Right away, the system tells us that adding a set to itself raises a TypeError exception. Sometimes, running a quick experiment in the interactive shell is the fastest way to get information we want, but documentation is nice too.

Fortunately, Python has a very good documentation system that we can access straight from the interactive shell by calling the help function. We could pass any object as the parameter of the help function and it will print out that object's documentation for us. So, if we want to find out about functools.wraps, we just pass it to help using the following two commands and read all about it (refer to the following screenshot):

```
import functools
help(functools.wraps)
```

```
Help on function wraps in module functools:

wraps(wrapped, assigned=('__module__', '__name__', '__qualname__', '__doc__', '__annotations__'), updated=('__dict__',))
    Decorator factory to apply update_wrapper() to a wrapper function

    Returns a decorator that invokes update_wrapper() with the decorated
    function as the wrapper argument and the arguments to wraps() as the
    remaining arguments. Default arguments are as for update_wrapper().
    This is a convenience function to simplify applying partial() to
    update_wrapper().
(END)
```

The help function can also take the name of the object you want to read about instead of the object itself using the following code:

```
help('collections.defaultdict')
```

This format can save us the time of typing in an `import` statement in the interactive shell:

```
Help on class defaultdict in collections:

collections.defaultdict = class defaultdict(builtins.dict)
 |  defaultdict(default_factory[, ...]) --> dict with default factory
 |
 |  The default factory is called without arguments to produce
 |  a new value when a key is not present, in __getitem__ only.
 |  A defaultdict compares equal to a dict with the same items.
 |  All remaining arguments are treated the same as if they were
 |  passed to the dict constructor, including keyword arguments.
 |
 |  Method resolution order:
 |      defaultdict
 |      builtins.dict
 |      builtins.object
 |
 |  Methods defined here:
 |
 |  __copy__(...)
 |      D.copy() -> a shallow copy of D.
 |
 |  __getattribute__(self, name, /)
 |      Return getattr(self, name).
 |
 |  __init__(self, /, *args, **kwargs)
 |      Initialize self.  See help(type(self)) for accurate signature.
 |
 |  __missing__(...)
 |      __missing__(key) # Called by __getitem__ for missing key; pseudo-code:
 |      if self.default_factory is None: raise KeyError((key,))
 |      self[key] = value = self.default_factory()
 |      return value
 |
 |  __reduce__(...)
 |      Return state information for pickling.
 |
 |  __repr__(self, /)
 |      Return repr(self).
 |
 |  copy(...)
 |      D.copy() -> a shallow copy of D.
 |
 |  ----------------------------------------------------------------------
 |  Data descriptors defined here:
 |
 |  default_factory
 |      Factory for default value called by __missing__().
 |
 |  ----------------------------------------------------------------------
 |  Methods inherited from builtins.dict:
 |
:
```

The difference is that the `help` parameter is a string and not an expression that evaluates to the object we're interested in.

Installing packages with pip

In this section, we'll take a look at using Python's package manager to install and manage third-party code, and now, it's back to the operating system command line for us. We'll see how to easily install third-party code from the Python Package Index.

While Python comes with batteries included, that is, the Python standard library that's already installed contains a wide range of very useful features, there's still plenty of things it doesn't do. Odds are though that somebody somewhere has already invented the wheel for us and if so, we can probably find it in the Python Package Index.

The pip tool for packages

Python, from version 3.4 onwards, is installed with a tool called `pip`, which can interface with the Python Package Index to automatically find, download, and install Python packages. If you already know the name of the package you want, and you have permission to write into Python's library directory, then this relatively simple command will get it fully installed and ready to be used.

In this instance, we installed a package called `banknumber`, which checks if someone's bank number is a valid bank number or is just a random number. For this, just add the `python3 -m pip install banknumber` command and hit *Enter*; we'll get the information as shown in the following screenshot:

```
devesh@devesh-VirtualBox:~$ python3 -m pip install banknumber
Collecting banknumber
  Using cached banknumber-2.0.tar.gz
Building wheels for collected packages: banknumber
  Running setup.py bdist_wheel for banknumber ... done
  Stored in directory: /home/devesh/.cache/pip/wheels/18/3b/d6/0bac9d3123898ef2bafc1e882b62e83a495d80bfe7b34996c8
Successfully built banknumber
Installing collected packages: banknumber
Successfully installed banknumber-2.0
```

If we don't have permission to Python's library directory, never fear. Python will look for a second user-specific library directory and since that library directory belongs to us, we'll always be able to install packages there.

To tell pip that we want to install into our personal library directory, just add `--user` to the command right after `install`. In the following screenshot, we are installing the `requests` package into our personal directory:

```
devesh@devesh-VirtualBox:~$ python3 -m pip install --user requests
Collecting requests
  Using cached requests-2.18.1-py2.py3-none-any.whl
Collecting urllib3<1.22,>=1.21.1 (from requests)
  Using cached urllib3-1.21.1-py2.py3-none-any.whl
Collecting idna<2.6,>=2.5 (from requests)
  Using cached idna-2.5-py2.py3-none-any.whl
Collecting chardet<3.1.0,>=3.0.2 (from requests)
  Using cached chardet-3.0.4-py2.py3-none-any.whl
Collecting certifi>=2017.4.17 (from requests)
  Using cached certifi-2017.4.17-py2.py3-none-any.whl
Installing collected packages: urllib3, idna, chardet, certifi, requests
Successfully installed certifi-2017.4.17 chardet-3.0.4 idna-2.5 requests-2.18.1 urllib3-1.21.1
```

Managing installed packages

The `pip` tool can do more than just installing packages. It can also give us the following:

- A list of currently installed packages using the `-m pip list` command:

```
devesh@devesh-VirtualBox:~$ python3 -m pip list
amqp (1.4.9)
anyjson (0.3.3)
apturl (0.5.2)
banknumber (2.0)
beautifulsoup4 (4.4.1)
blinker (1.3)
Brlapi (0.6.4)
certifi (2017.4.17)
chardet (3.0.4)
checkbox-support (0.22)
click (6.7)
command-not-found (0.3)
cryptography (1.2.3)
```

- Upgrade currently installed packages to the newest version using the `-m pip install --upgrade` command:

```
devesh@devesh-VirtualBox:~$ python3 -m pip install --upgrade requests
Collecting requests
  Using cached requests-2.18.1-py2.py3-none-any.whl
Collecting certifi>=2017.4.17 (from requests)
  Using cached certifi-2017.4.17-py2.py3-none-any.whl
Collecting urllib3<1.22,>=1.21.1 (from requests)
  Using cached urllib3-1.21.1-py2.py3-none-any.whl
Collecting idna<2.6,>=2.5 (from requests)
  Using cached idna-2.5-py2.py3-none-any.whl
Collecting chardet<3.1.0,>=3.0.2 (from requests)
  Using cached chardet-3.0.4-py2.py3-none-any.whl
Installing collected packages: certifi, urllib3, idna, chardet, requests
Successfully installed certifi-2017.4.17 chardet-3.0.4 idna-2.5 requests-2.18.1 urllib3-1.21.1
```

- Uninstall packages that we don't need anymore using the `-m pip uninstall` command. For example, if we want to uninstall the `banknumber` package, we can do it by using the following command, shown in this screenshot:

```
devesh@devesh-VirtualBox:~$ python3 -m pip uninstall banknumber
Uninstalling banknumber-2.0:
  /home/devesh/.local/lib/python3.5/site-packages/banknumber-2.0.dist-info/DESCRIPTION.rst
  /home/devesh/.local/lib/python3.5/site-packages/banknumber-2.0.dist-info/INSTALLER
  /home/devesh/.local/lib/python3.5/site-packages/banknumber-2.0.dist-info/METADATA
  /home/devesh/.local/lib/python3.5/site-packages/banknumber-2.0.dist-info/RECORD
  /home/devesh/.local/lib/python3.5/site-packages/banknumber-2.0.dist-info/WHEEL
  /home/devesh/.local/lib/python3.5/site-packages/banknumber-2.0.dist-info/metadata.json
  /home/devesh/.local/lib/python3.5/site-packages/banknumber-2.0.dist-info/top_level.txt
  /home/devesh/.local/lib/python3.5/site-packages/banknumber/__init__.py
  /home/devesh/.local/lib/python3.5/site-packages/banknumber/__pycache__/__init__.cpython-35.pyc
  /home/devesh/.local/lib/python3.5/site-packages/banknumber/__pycache__/tests.cpython-35.pyc
  /home/devesh/.local/lib/python3.5/site-packages/banknumber/tests.py
Proceed (y/n)? y
  Successfully uninstalled banknumber-2.0
```

In short, it's a complete cross-platform management tool for Python packages.

 Some Python packages require that we be able to compile extensions written in the C programming language to install them, but fortunately that's becoming rare. Normally, if the compiled extension is required, pip will be able to find and install the proper precompiled version automatically. The majority of available packages are pure Python anyhow and don't require compilation.

The pip tool has many more great options and command-line switches, but what we've seen so far covers the common situations well. If you want to dig into it further, pip's `help` command will give you the details. For example, consider the following command:

```
pip help install
```

The preceding command prints out all the information you could possibly want about the `pip install` option:

```
  --root <dir>                Install everything relative to this alternate root directory.
  --prefix <dir>              Installation prefix where lib, bin and other top-level folders are placed
  --compile                   Compile py files to pyc
  --no-compile                Do not compile py files to pyc
  --no-use-wheel              Do not Find and prefer wheel archives when searching indexes and find-links locations. DEPRECATED in
                              favour of --no-binary.
  --no-binary <format_control>
                              Do not use binary packages. Can be supplied multiple times, and each time adds to the existing value.
                              Accepts either :all: to disable all binary packages, :none: to empty the set, or one or more package
                              names with commas between them. Note that some packages are tricky to compile and may fail to install
                              when this option is used on them.
  --only-binary <format_control>
                              Do not use source packages. Can be supplied multiple times, and each time adds to the existing value.
                              Accepts either :all: to disable all source packages, :none: to empty the set, or one or more package
                              names with commas between them. Packages without binary distributions will fail to install when this
                              option is used on them.
  --pre                       Include pre-release and development versions. By default, pip only finds stable versions.
  --no-clean                  Don't clean up build directories.
  --require-hashes            Require a hash to check each requirement against, for repeatable installs. This option is implied
                              when any package in a requirements file has a --hash option.

Package Index Options (including deprecated options):
  -i, --index-url <url>       Base URL of Python Package Index (default https://pypi.python.org/simple).
  --extra-index-url <url>     Extra URLs of package indexes to use in addition to --index-url.
  --no-index                  Ignore package index (only looking at --find-links URLs instead).
  -f, --find-links <url>      If a url or path to an html file, then parse for links to archives. If a local path or file:// url
                              that's a directory, then look for archives in the directory listing.
  --process-dependency-links  Enable the processing of dependency links.

General Options:
  -h, --help                  Show help.
  --isolated                  Run pip in an isolated mode, ignoring environment variables and user configuration.
  -v, --verbose               Give more output. Option is additive, and can be used up to 3 times.
  -V, --version               Show version and exit.
  -q, --quiet                 Give less output.
  --log <path>                Path to a verbose appending log.
  --proxy <proxy>             Specify a proxy in the form [user:passwd@]proxy.server:port.
  --retries <retries>         Maximum number of retries each connection should attempt (default 5 times).
  --timeout <sec>             Set the socket timeout (default 15 seconds).
  --exists-action <action>    Default action when a path already exists: (s)witch, (i)gnore, (w)ipe, (b)ackup.
  --trusted-host <hostname>   Mark this host as trusted, even though it does not have valid or any HTTPS.
  --cert <path>               Path to alternate CA bundle.
  --client-cert <path>        Path to SSL client certificate, a single file containing the private key and the certificate in PEM
                              format.
  --cache-dir <dir>           Store the cache data in <dir>.
  --no-cache-dir              Disable the cache.
  --disable-pip-version-check
                              Don't periodically check PyPI to determine whether a new version of pip is available for download.
                              Implied with --no-index.
You are using pip version 8.1.1, however version 9.0.1 is available.
You should consider upgrading via the 'pip install --upgrade pip' command.
devesh@devesh-VirtualBox:~$
```

So, now that we know how to install third-party packages using `pip`, how do we go about actually finding packages to install in the first place?

Finding packages in the Python Package Index

Earlier, we talked about installing packages from the Python Package Index, but what if we don't have a specific package we need to install? What if we just need a library to help us get the job done, but don't know which specific one we need? Well, as the name of the section implies, the Python Package Index is actually an index of packages, which classifies the packages according to a number of parameters. The index is conveniently hosted at `https://pypi.python.org/pypi`. We could search the available packages in a number of ways. Let's discuss it in detail.

Using keywords

Perhaps, the most useful way of accessing the index is to simply type keywords into the search box and see what it spits out.

If we ask to search for `asyncio`, we get back a collection of package names that have something to do with `asyncio`. The names are, of course, links to each package's detailed description on the index, which we can use to decide which package best suits our needs.

There's another way of accessing the index that is often nearly as useful as keyword searching and sometimes even more useful.

Using Package Index

The Python Package Index supports browsing through its **Package Index** by category.

You start browsing by clicking on the **Browse packages** link in the menu, which brings you to the list of different categories. From there, you can select one or more categories by clicking on them and you'll be shown a list of the packages that fall into all of your selected categories, if the list is short enough to be useful.

 If you don't get a list of packages, it's because the list would be so long that it wouldn't do you any good and you should select more categories to narrow it down. If a category disappears from the list while you're selecting, it means that there are no packages that run all your selected categories.

Python is not only written in English or used by people who prefer this language, but some packages also have good support for other languages. This list is a good way to find them, whereas keyword searching might not pick up on that kind of detail.

Searching the Package Index with pip

If we don't want to fire up our browser to go searching through the index, we can also do it from the command line through `pip`, as shown in the following command:

```
$ python3 -m pip search asyncio
```

This command performs the same search that we did earlier through the web interface:

```
aiokafka (0.2.2)              - Kafka integration with asyncio.
ws (0.1)                      - Efficient asyncio based web crawler
aiowerkzeug (0.2.0)           - Werkzeug for asyncio
camisole (0.5)                - An asyncio-based source compiler and test runner.
jsonrpc-async (0.6)           - A JSON-RPC client library for asyncio
aioopenssl (0.3.1)            - TLS-capable transport using OpenSSL for asyncio
aioweb (0.1)                  - Asynchronous web framework, based on asyncio
mocket (1.8.2)                - Socket Mock Framework - for all kinds of socket animals, web-clients included -
                                with gevent/asyncio/SSL support
shampoo (0.1.0b12)            - Shampoo is a asyncio websocket protocol implementation for Autobahn
butter (0.12.6)               - Library to interface to low level linux features (inotify, fanotify, timerfd, signalfd
                                eventfd, containers) with asyncio support
aio_periodic (0.1.6)          - The periodic task system client for python3 base on asyncio
aiohttp_jinja2 (0.13.0)       - jinja2 template renderer for aiohttp.web (http server for asyncio)
subconscious (0.8.5)          - redis-backed db for python3 (asyncio compatible)
thriftasyncioserver (0.1.7)   - Thrift Server using the Python 3 asyncio module
asyncrest (1.0.1)             - RESTful helper for asyncio
aioirc (0.1)                  - AsyncIO IRC Library for >= Python 3.3
```

Doing it this way is often faster; but as you can see in the preceding screenshot, it only provides us with a name and a brief description of each package. This is perfect for getting a quick reminder about the package name, but not so good for more in-depth research.

Legalities and licenses of the Python Package Index

Finally, a quick note about legalities and licenses!

The vast majority of packages in the Python Package Index are under open-source licenses as certified by the **Open Source Institute (OSI)**. This means basically that they can be freely used and distributed as part of other open-source projects.

In most cases, the licenses are more liberal than this, allowing us to use the software as part of our projects, even if we don't open source our own code.

 Most does not mean all, however some of the packages are not under OSI certified licenses and some of OSI licensed packages are not usable in closed-source projects.

So, if you're going to be distributing your software, take a moment to make sure the licenses line up with your goals.

Summary

In this chapter, we learned how to install Python and get to a place where we can begin working on real code. We looked at running Python in a command-line window and using it to perform experiments and calculations. We examined how to make the best of Python's command line and its extensive `help` library.

We learned about installing, uninstalling, and upgrading the packages using `pip`. We also got a pretty good idea of how to find third-party code to help us move our projects along, using the Python Package Index.

In the next chapter, we'll work through the steps to create and work with our own Python code packages.

3
Making a Package

In the previous chapter, we saw how to install Python and third-party packages of code that we can use with Python. In this chapter, we'll see how packages are represented on the computer's filesystem. We'll take a look at how to add code modules inside the package, how to make those code modules interact with each other within the package, and how to access data from non-code files that are incorporated into our package.

By the end of this chapter, you'll have a pretty good idea about how to create your own packages of Python code. Packages will form the basis for programs and help you to make your code modular.

In this chapter, we will cover the following topics:

- Creating an empty package
- Adding modules to the package
- Accessing code from other modules
- Adding static data files to the package

Creating an empty package

The first section of this chapter deals with creating a simple empty package, which won't do anything yet, but by the time we're done, we'll be able to import the empty package into the Python shell.

Simple Python projects may consist of a single code module, but normally there are multiple modules combined together into a package. A package can contain as many modules as we need it to. Packages start their lives as folders on the filesystem, which means we can make them just as we would make any other folder.

If you prefer to use your operating system's file browser to make folders, that's fine, but I usually use the command line. For example let's run a demo package:

```
$ mkdir demopackage
```

This is shown as the following screenshot:

```
devesh@devesh-VirtualBox:~$ mkdir demopackage
devesh@devesh-VirtualBox:~$ python3
```

Turning a regular folder into a package

There are two things that turn a regular folder into a package. These are explained as follows:

The first is *where is it* that is, the location of the folder. Python only looks in certain places for packages and if your folder isn't in the right place, Python won't notice it.

The sys.path variable contains the list of all the places Python will look for packages. The sys.path variable is fairly sparse, but user configuration can make it much more extensive as shown in the following screenshot:

```
>>> import sys
>>> sys .path
['', '/usr/lib/python35.zip', '/usr/lib/python3.5', '/usr/lib/python3.5/plat-x86_64-linux-gnu', '/u
sr/local/lib/python3.5/dist-packages', '/usr/lib/python3/dist-packages']
>>>
```

Notice that the first entry in the list is an empty string. This stands for the current working directory.

For those who are using the command line, the current working directory is just the folder we're currently in.

We can change the current working directory with the cd command:

```
cd demopackage
cd ..
```

The `cd..` command in the preceding code means go back to the previous directory or the parent directory. So, in this case, I went in and out of `demopackage`.

The fact that the current working directory is in the path is convenient during development; it means that we could just set the current working directory to the place where we're doing our development and all of our packages become available, at least, as long as we also use the command line to launch Python.

The second thing that turns a regular folder into a package is the presence of __init__.py file, though not strictly necessary since Python 3.3 and beyond. An `init` file marks the folder as a package, which makes it load more efficiently and also gives us a place to put information and code relevant to the interface of the package as a whole.

While it's quite common that the __init__.py file is completely empty and serves only as a marker, there's one language feature that won't be supported unless we add a little code to the file.

This feature is the ability to import all the package's modules using the `import *` syntax, as shown here:

```
>>> import demopackage
>>> exit()
devesh@devesh-VirtualBox:~$ emacs demopackage/__init__.py
```

Importing all package modules

If we want Python to be able to import all the package's modules using `import *` syntax, we have to tell it the names of all those modules.

To do this, we add the module names to a list called __all__ in the init file as shown in the following code:

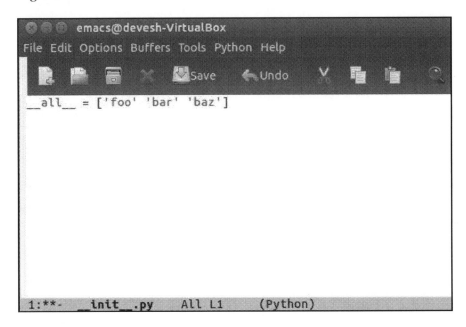

If you don't have *emacs* installed on your system, you can install it by using the following command:

`sudo apt install emacs24`

In the preceding screenshot, I have used Ubuntu, thus the editor is white background, however in case of Windows OS and macOS, the background of the editor can be different.

You might be wondering why we need to do this manually rather than Python just scanning the filesystem for module files.

Well, there are a couple of reasons:

- First, Python tries not to make any assumptions about whether filenames are case-sensitive or not. On some operating systems, filenames are case-sensitive and on other operating systems they are not. Module names are variables, so it's better they originate within the source code, rather than depending on something external that might change depending on where the code is run.

- The second reason for doing this manually is that importing a module makes code execute.

Imagine we have a package that plays soundtracks. In addition to the general purpose code, we also have a bunch of modules that handle audio output on various systems.

Allowing our users to do an `import *` to bring their packages' programming interface into their module is quite reasonable; however, we don't want all of the output modules to load, just the one that's appropriate to the system we're running on. Trying to load any of the others would most likely trigger an exception in the user's code. The way `__all__` works now, we can exclude the output modules from `import *` and get the best of both worlds.

Alright, let's make sure that Python is willing to import our demo package before we move on to the next part, which is how to add source code modules to a package.

Adding modules to the package

Now, let's take look at how to add actual code to the package and look out for a couple of pitfalls to avoid.

Python modules have the same name as objects that they have as filenames, except without the `.py` suffix. This means that the filenames need to be valid Python variable names and also that they should use letters and symbols that are reliably available across different operating systems. The following screenshot showns an example for this:

```
devesh@devesh-VirtualBox:~$ ls
demo    demo2       Desktop    Downloads           __init__.py  Pictures  Templates
demo1   demopackage Documents  examples.desktop    Music                  Public    Videos
devesh@devesh-VirtualBox:~$
```

So, module names should not start with a number because Python variables are not allowed to start with numbers. Also, it should not use capital letters because some common operating system don't differentiate between filenames containing capital letters and filenames that are all lowercase. As long as we stay within Python variable name guidelines and remember to use a `.py` suffix, we can name our modules anything we please.

So, we just pick a filename and start writing Python code into a file with that name in the `package` folder. That simple scenario is also the common case, but there's another possibility.

Module loading with namespace packages

As mentioned earlier, starting with Python 3.3, it's possible to have a `package` folder that doesn't contain an `init` file. Leaving out the `init` file means we can't support `import *` or the other tricks within it that we'll discover as we go along. But, there's more to it than that. The following screenshot shows a code example for this:

```
devesh@devesh-VirtualBox:~$ mkdir demo1
devesh@devesh-VirtualBox:~$ mkdir demo1/nsdemo
devesh@devesh-VirtualBox:~$ touch demo1/nsdemo/foo.py
devesh@devesh-VirtualBox:~$ mkdir demo2
devesh@devesh-VirtualBox:~$ mkdir demo2/nsdemo
devesh@devesh-VirtualBox:~$ touch demo2/nsdemo/bar.py
devesh@devesh-VirtualBox:~$ ls -lR *
-rw-r--r-- 1 devesh devesh 8980 Jun 20 11:18 examples.desktop
-rw-rw-r-- 1 devesh devesh   30 Jun 20 11:54 __init__.py

demo1:
total 4
drwxrwxr-x 2 devesh devesh 4096 Jun 20 13:25 nsdemo

demo1/nsdemo:
total 0
-rw-rw-r-- 1 devesh devesh 0 Jun 20 13:25 foo.py

demo2:
total 4
drwxrwxr-x 2 devesh devesh 4096 Jun 20 13:25 nsdemo

demo2/nsdemo:
total 0
-rw-rw-r-- 1 devesh devesh 0 Jun 20 13:25 bar.py

demopackage:
total 4
-rw-rw-r-- 1 devesh devesh 30 Jun 20 13:22 __init__.py
```

When the `init` file is missing, the folder becomes part of a `namespace package` folder. When Python is importing, it combines all of the `namespace package` folders it finds, that share a name, into a single logical package, as shown in the following screenshot:

```
>>> import sys
>>> sys.path.append('demo1')
>>> sys.path.append('demo2')
>>> from nsdemo import foo, bar
>>>
```

This behavior means that while choosing the module filename, Python still follows the same rules, we could potentially place that file into one of any number of `namespace package` folders instead of into a singular concrete `package` folder.

What do we gain from that? Often nothing!

As I mentioned earlier, packages with an `init` load faster, and in many cases, the extra abstraction of namespace packages doesn't buy us anything.

There are cases, however, when we want different parts of the same package to be distributed or managed separately and when we do, `namespace packages` address that need. For example, imagine again that we are working on a package for playing soundtracks. If we make a `namespace package` folder for audio codecs, each codec could be installed and removed individually using `pip` or the operating system's normal package management tools.

On a slightly different topic, now let's talk about the difference between how a package is structured and the interface it should present for use by external code.

The Package structure and interface

For the convenience and sanity of ourselves as the package developers, it's often best to break up the code in a package into many different modules, all of which contain a selection of conceptually related code; this is the package's structure. As a rule of thumb, whenever we think we might want to break the code up into more modules, we probably should go with that impulse.

On the other hand, external code calling on our package is best off when it can take advantage of our code with just one or two import statements that bring in a small number of functions or classes. This is the package's interface, and as a rule of thumb, it should be as minimal as possible, while preserving full functionality, as shown in the following code example:

```
from example.foo import Foo
from example.bar import BarFactory
from example.baz import Baz

MAIN_BAZ = BAZ()

__all__ = ['Foo', 'BarFactory', 'MAIN_BAZ']
```

Fortunately, we can have our cake and eat it too!

We could divide our code up however we wish and then import the most useful elements into our init file, which will make them part of the package's route namespace. If all that's in an init file is import statements, we don't need the __all__ variable.

An import* statement will grab the contents of the init file except for variables, starting with an underscore. However, if we define or import anything in the init file that should not be part of the public interface, we can use the __all__ variable to narrow down and control what we export.

Just remember, if we have an all list, it needs to list everything that is part of the package's interface, whether a module, class, function, or variable.

The rest of the modules in the package are still available to be explicitly imported. We're just making it convenient to access the parts that are most likely to be useful outside our own package.

Now we have a good idea of how to name our modules, where to put them so that they become part of our package, and how to give our package a convenient interface. Next, we'll move on to looking at how to make the modules in a package interact with each other.

Accessing code from other modules

We'll start off this section by understanding the difference between absolute and relative imports, then move on to writing those, and finally, we'll look at cyclic dependencies.

When we are importing one of the package's modules from outside the package, there's only one sensible way that it could work-we tell Python which package and module we want, and it either finds and imports it or raises an exception if it can't. Simple!

```
import packagename.modulename
```

When we're already inside a package, the situation is more ambiguous because `import name` could just as easily mean "look for `name` within this package" or "look for `name` in the Python search path." Python breaks this ambiguity by defining `import name` to mean that a package or module called **name** should be searched for in Python's search path:

```
import name
```

Also, it also gives us a way to specify a relative `import` if we'd rather have it just look within the current package. We can specify a relative `import` by putting a dot in front of the name of the module we want to import, as shown in the following code:

```
import .name
```

When Python sees this, it will look for a module called `name` in the same package as the module our code is running in.

Often, we only need one or two objects from another module and it's more convenient to import those objects directly into our global scope than it would be to import the module as a whole and access its contents. Python lets us do that with a slight variation on the `import` syntax:

```
from .name import Foo
```

Finally, sometimes we want to rename an object within our scope as we import it. We could do that by modifying our import with the `as` keyword:

```
from .name import Foo as Bar
```

In the preceding example, even though the object is called Foo in the name module, in our current module, it's named Bar. This trick works for absolute imports too by the way.

 Before we move on, let's take note that Python 2 used a different rule for deciding where to find imported code. In Python 2, it first tried to find a target of an import within the current package. Then, if no matching module was found there, it went out and looked for it on the search path. This approach usually did the right thing, but occasionally caused problems due to the ambiguous meaning; and it meant that we couldn't have some packages, sub-packages, or modules that shared the name of anything in the standard library or other installed packages. So, this behavior was changed in Python 3.

Importing a cyclic dependency

There is something that might trip us up when we're importing a module that shares the same package. Sometimes, the module we're importing wants to import us as well. This is called a **cyclic dependency**. When we try to import a cyclic dependency, we'll almost always get an attribute error exception, as in the following example:

```python
import .b

class A:
    def __init__(self):
        print(str(self))

class C(b.B):
    def __str__(self):
        return 'C'
```

```python
import .a

class B(a.A):
    def __str__(self):
        return 'B'
```

That happens because when we ask Python to import the first module, Python immediately creates a module object for it and begins executing the code in the module.

That's fine, except that, when Python gets to the import statement for the next module in this cycle, it pauses running the code in the first module, leaving it not fully initialized. Even that isn't normally a problem because Python will come back and finish the initialization later.

However, when the second module asks to import the first module, Python just hands it the already allocated, and not fully initialized, module object. When the second module tries to access the variables stored in the first object, many of them will not yet have been created. Hence, an attribute error is raised.

Resolving attribute errors raised due to cyclic dependencies

There are two common ways to address the attribute error. The first one is usually considered the best. This method is to break the cycle by taking some of the code from one of the modules and moving it into a third module, which both the other modules can import without causing a cycle. In the following example, if we move the A class into its own module, there would be no cycle and all would be well:

```
# a.py                               import .a

class A:                             class B(a.A):
    def __init__(self):                  def __str__(self):
        print(str(self))                     return 'B'

# b.py

import .b
class C(b.B):
    def __str__(self):
        return 'C'
```

The other way to address this problem is to move the import statement that causes the cycle, as shown in the following screenshot:

```
class A:                             import .a
    def __init__(self):
        print(str(self))             class B(a.A):
                                         def __str__(self):
                                             return 'B'
import .b

class C(b.B):
    def __str__(self):
        return 'C'
```

If we move the import statement down, as shown in the preceding example, until it's below all the variable definitions that are needed by the other modules in this cycle, the module will be initialized enough when it's imported by the other modules. Python will still come back and finish the initialization later.

Adding static data files to the package

If we're going to add static data files to the package, where should we put them?

Well we can put them anywhere that's convenient within the package folder, but it's often a good idea to create a subfolder specifically for holding the data files. This keeps data files separate from the source code and generally makes them a little easier to work with.

 The data files that are part of a package should be assumed to be read-only.

There are many reasons that might cause the files to not be writable at runtime. So, if we want to write data to a file while our code is running, we need to pick somewhere else to store it. Only files that do not change are appropriate for inclusion in a package:

```
ls example/
__init__.py data
ls example/data
datafile.txt
cat example/data/datafile.txt
Hello world of data
```

So, that said, all we have to do to include a data file in our package is drop it into our package and then access the data with the get_data function from the util package in the standard library:

```
from pkgutil import get_data
get_data('example', 'data/datafile.txt')
b'Hello world of data\n'
```

The get_data function takes two parameters:

- The name of the package we want to get the data from
- The relative path of the data file inside the package

Using forward slashes to separate path components, we pass it these two pieces of information and it returns a byte object to us containing the contents of the file.

If we want a text string instead of bytes, that's easily done. We just need to apply the proper string decoder to the bytes object and we'll get back a unicode text string. This technique will work even if our package has been compressed into a ZIP file or otherwise hidden away because it uses the same underlying mechanism that Python uses to load module source code.

If Python can find the code, it can find the data file as well. That's all there is to working with static data that's packaged up alongside our code. It's simple and useful.

Summary

In this chapter, we learned how to create a Python package as a directory on the filesystem and how to mark it with an __init__.py file, so that importing is efficient and we can add package metadata. We looked at adding code modules to a package. We saw how code modules within the same package interact.

We learned how to put together a Python code package that can be used in a program or distributed to other programmers. Soon, we'll see how to turn a package into a complete program as well. In the next chapter, we'll step back a little bit and talk about some best practices for working with Python code.

4
Basic Best Practices

In the previous chapter, we saw how to put together a Python package of code and data. In this chapter, we're going to look at some rather simple things we can do that will make our lives as Python programmers simpler overall. We'll switch gears and look at version control, which will help us to collaborate with other programmers and serve as an undo buffer for the whole lifetime of a project. We're going to look at Python's built-in virtual environment tool, venv, which allows us to keep our programs and dependencies separate from each other and the software installed on our overall system.

You'll learn how to structure our docstrings for maximum utility, how to add Rich Text formatting to them, and how to export them into hyperlinked HTML documentation for viewing in a web browser. You'll also see one more cool advantage we can get from docstrings by actually executing the examples we include in our documentation and making sure they agree with what the code actually does.

In this chapter, we'll cover the following topics:

- PEP 8 and writing readable code
- Using version control
- Using venv to create a stable and isolated work area
- Getting the most out of docstrings

PEP 8 and writing readable code

In this section, we'll take a quick look at how to format our code so that it'll be easy to read when we come back to it at some later date or when somebody else has to work with it. We will specifically take a look at indentation rules, the Python code style guide, and finally, the standard naming convention.

Python Enhancement Proposals or **PEPs** are the documents that establish standards in the Python community. Most PEPs describe new features for Python or Python's standard library, but a few of them are more nebulous. PEP 8 is one of those; it tells us what the Python community considers to be well-written, readable code.

PEP 8 — guidelines for Python code

The very first rule PEP 8 introduces is that rules/guidelines in PEP 8 should only apply when they make our code easier to read. This means we should apply PEP 8 to enhance the readability of the code and to make it less complex. For example, if we're working on a project that was already written with a different coding style (that is, it is already easy to read), we should use that project style for new code. If the PEP 8 rules somehow make the code harder to read or make it complex while writing the code, we should ignore those rules. As Guido Van Rossum, the creator of Python, has noted:

Code is read more often than it is written.

 Code should always be written in a way that promotes readability.

For more information on PEP 8 rules and guidelines, you can refer to the following link: `https://www.python.org/dev/peps/pep-0008/`.

To know when to ignore a particular guideline, you can follow the *A Foolish Consistency is the Hobgoblin of Little Minds* article at the following link: `https://www.python.org/dev/peps/pep-0008/#a-foolish-consistency-is-the-hobgoblin-of-little-minds`.

Code indentation

As programmers, when we read code we look at how it's indented to tell us how the code blocks are nested. However, most other programming languages use actual symbols to tell the language parser where a block begins and ends. In coding, the same information in two different places is a violation of the basic best practices of any programming language. So, Python omits the beginning and ending block markers and uses indentation (as shown in the following code screenshot) to inform the parser as well as the programmer:

```python
def tabs_cause_problem():
    with open('test.txt') as f:
        for line in f:
            try:
                print(int(line))
            except ValueError:
                print('Not an integer')
```

There is one problem that arises from that, though!

There are different ways of encoding indentation in a text file. These are as follows:

- Use Space characters
- Tab characters
- A combination of both

The codes we're looking at in the preceding code image mixes spaces and tabs, which, in Python 2 was valid, but a terrible idea, and which, in Python 3, is a syntax error. I've configured the editor to highlight tab characters in color, so we can easily see which indentation comes from spaces and which comes from tabs, to see why mixing spaces and tabs is not good, even when it's allowed.

All we have to do is change the tab width and it will look something like the following code image:

```python
def tabs_cause_problem():
    with open('test.txt') as f:
for line in f:
        try:
    print(int(line))
        except ValueError:
    print('Not an integer')
```

Even though the indentation looked good in the previous code image, now it's clearly wrong. There's no ambiguity if all indentation comes from tab characters. So, using only tabs is valid, even in Python 3. However, it is the recommendation of PEP 8 and the Python community that we always use exactly four spaces to indicate one level of indentation. Any halfway decent editor can insert those spaces for us when we press the **Tab** key. There are several more recommendations, which we're going to go through quickly in the next sub-section.

Formatting recommendations

The code in the following screenshot demonstrates almost all the PEP 8 formatting recommendations:

```python
"""Demonstrate PEP 8 layout

This module does nothing useful, aside from demonstrating most of the
layout rules of PEP 8.
"""

import sys
import re
from pickle import loads, dumps

class Elephant:
    """Tracks elephants and their optional associated dormice.

    """
    def __init__(self, dormouse = None):
        """Create an Elephant, and optionally tie it to a DorMouse.

        If specified, the dormouse parameter should be a DorMouse
        instance which should be associated with this Elephant.

        """
        self.dormouse = dormouse

        if dormouse:
            dormouse.set_elephant(self)


class DorMouse:
    """Tracks dormice, optionally associated with elephants.

    Each DorMouse instance has the ability to associate with 0 or 1
```

```python
def munge(left, right):
    """Make a horrible mess.

    This function takes a pair of ScarePair objects and twists them up
    into a pretzel.

    """
    left[1].set_elephant(right[0])
    right[1].set_elephant(left[0])

    new_left = (left[0], right[1])
    new_right = (right[0], left[1])

    return new_left, new_right
```

I'll now walk us through the recommendations one by one:

- PEP 8 recommends that a single line of code should not exceed a width of 79 characters

 While this is consistent with displaying the code on a standard text mode interface, the primary reason for this rule in the modern world of widescreens and resizable windows is that it helps with reading. Even in contexts that have nothing to do with programming, layout designers prefer to limit line width.

- Import statements should be placed at the top of the file, with standard library imports first, third-party imports next, and then imports from other modules within the same project
- There should be a blank line between each group of imports
- Classes and functions at the top level should have two blank lines separating them.
- Methods within a class should have one blank line separating them
- Within a function or method, blank lines should be used to indicate separation between conceptual groupings of code
- Don't insert extra spaces before or after parentheses, brackets, or braces; and don't insert spaces before commas or colons
- Always put a single space on either side of a binary operator, such as + or /
- Don't put more than one statement on the same line, which is occasionally possible, but never a good idea
- Comments should be written in human language, using that language's correct grammar

 Preferably, that language should be English if you're going to allow your source code into the wild because this language is common to the majority of Python programmers.

- Comments should also precede the section of code they described and be indented to the same level
- Every public module, class, function, or method should have a properly formatted docstring

 We'll look at what properly formatted means for docstrings in the *Getting the most out of docstrings* section of this chapter.

Let's move on to picking names for variables, functions, methods, classes, modules, packages, and so on.

Naming conventions

The overriding rule of Python naming conventions is that the naming style for an object should make it plain how the object is used, not what the object is underneath. This means, for example, that a top-level function, which is called to create new objects and which therefore behaves like a class, should be named like a class.

- **Packages and modules**: These should have reasonably short names consisting entirely of lowercase letters, and in the case of modules, underscores.
- **Classes**: These should be named with a capitalized first letter and capitals at the start of every new word within the name. This is sometimes also called camel case. Exceptions should be classes and so they should follow the class naming convention, but they should also end with the word `Error`.
- **Functions**, **methods**, **instance variables**, and **global variables**: These all should be lower case, with underscores separating the words. If they are meant to be internal rather than part of the public interface, their names should begin with a single underscore.
    - The first parameter of an instance method should always be named self. Named **constant** values should be written in all capital letters, with underscores separating the words.

That's it for PEP 8 and the formatting rules that most Python programmers expect other people's code to follow. Now, let's move on to talking about nuts and bolts with a discussion of version control.

Using version control

Version control is one of the fundamental tools for programmers in the modern world. It helps us with almost every aspect of a project, in one way or another. There are many version control systems and each of them is a topic in itself, so we're going to narrow our focus here and talk about how to do a few particularly useful things, using a specific version control system called Git.

Initializing Git

The first thing we need to do to use Git, after installing it of course, is to set up a folder as our `Git repository`. This only takes a couple of commands on the command line, as shown here:

```
$ git init
Initialized empty Git repository in /home/djarb/tmp/gitdemo/.git/
$ echo "moo cow" > file.txt
$ git add file.txt
```

After that, we move to the folders where we want the repository to be, that is, `git init` and `git add`. Once we've initialized the repository, we add any files that we've already created to it with the `git add` command. Then, we create our first safe point in the code with the `git commit -a` command, as shown here:

```
git commit -a
```

Committing the changes in Git

The `git commit -a` commit command tells Git to commit all the changes that have been made:

```
File  Edit  Options  Buffers  Tools  Help
First commit
# Please enter the commit message for your changes. Lines starting
# with '#' will be ignored, and an empty message aborts the commit.
# On branch master
#
# Initial commit
#
# Changes to be committed:
#     new file:    file.txt
#
```

In the future, if we add new files to the project, we should also use `git add` to tell Git to start tracking them. Any time you want Git to remember the current state of our project, we run `git commit -a` again.

Undoing the changes

The nice thing about having old project states saved away is that we can go back to them.

For example, let's say we have made some changes in our `file.txt` file from `moo cow` to `moo aardvark`, as shown in the following screenshots:

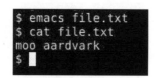

If we want to revert a file to a previous state, undoing everything we've done to that file since a particular commit, we just use the `git log` command to find the identifier for that commit:

```
git log
```

This will lead us to our commit, as shown here:

```
commit a0e436ee4fc347463088a0a804f0085c97879a52
Author: Daniel Arbuckle <djarb@highenergymagic.org>
Date:   Fri Sep 30 08:19:26 2016 -0700

    First commit
lines 1-5/5 (END)
```

Then, we use the `git checkout` command to undo our changes. To use the `git checkout` command, we just need to enter the commit and the filename and you will get to undo the changes, as shown here:

```
$ git checkout a0e436ee4fc347463088a0a804f0085c97879a52 file.txt
$ cat file.txt
moo cow
```

If we later change our minds, we can redo the changes in the same way. The ability to undo on the project level is great, but it's even more useful to make provisional changes to our code and then decide, once the changes are done, whether or not we really want them in our main code. That's what branches are for.

Branches

We can make a new branch with `git checkout -b`, which will create the branch and switch to it automatically:

```
$ git checkout -b feature
Switched to a new branch 'feature'
```

When we're in the branch, any code changes we make are associated with a branch, and when we leave the branch, they go away. This can be shown in the following example.

Let's say we want to change the `moo cow` to `moo horse`. For this, we'll run the following command to open up Emacs and edit the text file:

```
$ emacs file.txt
```

We'll then make the changes we want in the file:

We can then commit the file to the branch using the `git commit -a` command and add a commit message to keep track of the changes that we've made:

```
File  Edit  Options  Buffers  Tools  Help
It's a horse now
# Please enter the commit message for your changes. Lines starting
# with '#' will be ignored, and an empty message aborts the commit.
# On branch feature
# Changes to be committed:
#       modified:   file.txt
#
```

You'll see a record of those changes to show what's been committed:

```
$ git commit -a
[feature 7550b32] It's a horse now
 1 file changed, 1 insertion(+), 1 deletion(-)
```

You can then switch back to the master version using the `git checkout master` command to see the original files without any changes, and when we re-enter the branch, those changes come back:

```
$ git checkout master
Switched to branch 'master'
```

This means that we can still work on bug fixes in our main branch while we are working on new features in their own development branches. For example, here we can enter the same text file and change the animal to a dog, leaving a comment explaining what we've done:

```
File   Edit   Options   Buffers   Tools   Text   YASnippet   Help
moo dog # just a bugfix, will be replaced by new features later
```

Then, when we commit that file, we'll also leave a message stating that we've just made a bugfix:

```
File   Edit   Options   Buffers   Tools   Help
Bugfix
# Please enter the commit message for your changes. Lines starting
# with '#' will be ignored, and an empty message aborts the commit.
# On branch master
# Changes to be committed:
#       modified:   file.txt
#
```

As always, we commit the file using the `git commit` -a command, and we are shown a record of the changes, as follows:

```
$ git commit -a
[master 1c5b16b] Bugfix
 1 file changed, 1 insertion(+), 1 deletion(-)
```

When we're finally happy with a feature, we can merge it into the main branch.

Merging codes

To merge code from a different branch, all we have to do is to use the `git merge` command from inside the branch we're merging to and give it the name of the branch we're merging from. If the two branches cannot be automatically combined, Git will do it for us:

```
$ git log
$ cat file.txt
moo dog # just a bugfix, will be replaced by new features later
$ git checkout feature
Switched to branch 'feature'
$ cat file.txt
moo horse
$ git checkout master
Switched to branch 'master'
$ git merge feature
Auto-merging file.txt
CONFLICT (content): Merge conflict in file.txt
Automatic merge failed; fix conflicts and then commit the result.
$
```

That's usually all there is to it, but sometimes there are overlapping changes in both branches; when that happens, Git knows it's not smart enough to handle the merger on its own.

When we run `git merge`, it will notify us that there are conflicts. Then, we can use `git mergetool` to start up the merge resolution tool:

```
$ git mergetool

This message is displayed because 'merge.tool' is not configured.
See 'git mergetool --tool-help' or 'git help config' for more details.
'git mergetool' will now attempt to use one of the following tools:
opendiff kdiff3 tkdiff xxdiff meld tortoisemerge gvimdiff diffuse diffmerge
f
Merging:
file.txt

Normal merge conflict for 'file.txt':
  {local}: modified file
  {remote}: modified file
Hit return to start merge resolution tool (meld):
```

The mergetool command

The merge resolution tool lets us use our greater intelligence to resolve the conflict, as shown here:

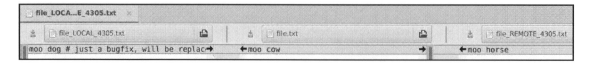

The `moo cow` should be changed to `moo horse` to avoid the conflict:

After the required changes, go to **File** and quit the interface.

Once that's done, we use the `git commit` command to finalize our changes, as shown in the following screenshot.

```
Normal merge conflict for 'file.txt':
  {local}: modified file
  {remote}: modified file
Hit return to start merge resolution tool (meld):

(meld:4397): Gtk-WARNING **: Failed to measure available space: Error getting filesystem info: Function not implemented

(meld:4397): Gtk-WARNING **: Failed to measure available space: Error getting filesystem info: Function not implemented

(meld:4397): Gtk-WARNING **: Failed to measure available space: Error getting filesystem info: Function not implemented

(meld:4397): Gtk-WARNING **: Failed to measure available space: Error getting filesystem info: Function not implemented

(meld:4397): Gtk-WARNING **: Failed to measure available space: Error getting filesystem info: Function not implemented

(meld:4397): Gtk-WARNING **: Failed to measure available space: Error getting filesystem info: Function not implemented
$ git commit
[master b4f7985] Merge branch 'feature'
$ git branch
  feature
* master
$ cat file.txt
moo horse
```

The `mergetool` command is a smart command that looks for several different tools that exist on various operating systems and picks one of them that it hopes is the best choice for you.

In the present case, it has picked a tool called `meld`, which is also written in Python incidentally, for me to use to fix the ambiguity.

The pull command

Git can do something very similar to combine code from other repositories into our own. The command for that is `git pull`, rather than `git merge`, and instead of a branch name, we provide the URL or pathname to a different repository, as shown here:

```
$ git pull http://www.somewhere.net/path/to/something.git
```

But otherwise, it functions in the same way. This is an incredibly useful feature because it allows us to easily collaborate with other coders, both locally and around the world.

Using venv to create a stable and isolated work area

When we're working on a project, we usually like the parts of the project that aren't our own code to stay the same. We might have a good reason to install a new version of Python or updated library on our system, but we don't really want those things to change within our development environment. Even more so, we can easily find ourselves targeting entirely different and incompatible system configurations with different projects. We need a way to set aside an area for each project that is separate and can be configured for the specific needs of that project. That's what we call a virtual environment.

The venv tool that's built in to Python 3.3, and later, creates a virtual environment for us. Each virtual environment created by venv knows which version of Python it should be using and has its own package library, which means that as far as Python code is concerned, it's basically disconnected from the rest of the system.

We can install, uninstall, and update packages on the system and the code inside the virtual environment won't even notice. We can install new versions of Python and the code inside the virtual environment won't notice. The only thing we can't safely do at the system level is uninstalling the version of Python that the virtual environment is based on.

Creating a virtual environment

Creating a virtual environment for a new project is easy; we just open the command line and go to the folder where we want the project folder to reside. Then, we use the version of Python that we want the virtual environment to use to run the venv tool:

```
$ python3.5 -m venv example
```

When we call venv, we tell it the name we want to give to the project folder. The venv tool will create the project folder and populate it with the files needed to support the virtual environment:

```
$ python3.5 -m venv example
$ cd example
$ ls
bin   include   lib   lib64   pyvenv.cfg
$
```

Each time we actually want to work inside the virtual environment, we should activate it. This will make whatever changes are needed, so that the contents of the virtual environment override the system-level defaults.

Activating a virtual environment

To activate a virtual environment, we open a command line and go to the folder containing the virtual environment:

```
$ source bin/activate
(example) $
```

Then, execute the activation command. The specific activation command we're using depends on the operating system.

On most Unix-style systems, including Macintosh, we use the `$ source bin\activate` command (as shown in the preceding screengrab). On Windows, we run `Scripts\activate.bat`.

We are operating inside an activated virtual environment, pip automatically knows it should manage packages for that environment:

```
(example) $ pip install aiohttp
Collecting aiohttp
  Downloading aiohttp-1.0.2-cp35-cp35m-manylinux1_x86_64.whl (150kB)
    100% |                              | 153kB 3.0MB/s
Collecting multidict>=2.0 (from aiohttp)
  Downloading multidict-2.1.2-cp35-cp35m-manylinux1_x86_64.whl (340kB)
    100% |                              | 348kB 2.8MB/s
Collecting async-timeout (from aiohttp)
  Downloading async_timeout-1.0.0-py3-none-any.whl
Collecting chardet (from aiohttp)
  Downloading chardet-2.3.0.tar.gz (164kB)
    100% |                              | 174kB 4.5MB/s
Installing collected packages: multidict, async-timeout, chardet, aiohttp
  Running setup.py install for chardet ... done
Successfully installed aiohttp-1.0.2 async-timeout-1.0.0 chardet-2.3.0 multidict-2.1.2
You are using pip version 8.1.1, however version 8.1.2 is available.
You should consider upgrading via the 'pip install --upgrade pip' command.
(example) $ █
```

pip in virtual environments

Initially, the virtual environment contains only the Python standard library and a couple of utilities, including pip itself.

However, we can use `pip` to install the third-party packages that we're going to use on the project. When we looked at pip, you learned about its `--user` command-line option, which installs the package into a personal package library instead of the system library.

 Installing the package into a personal package library, instead of the system library, is never necessary when installing into a virtual environment because the virtual environment has changed where the default installation location is.

Now that everything is set up, we can begin work. We shouldn't delete any of the files or folders created by venv or pip. However, other than that, we're free to create files and folders as needed for our project. It is often useful to create a subdirectory to contain our working code.

Now that you learned how to use the simple, but useful, venv tool to isolate our coding projects from each other and from most changes to our development system, let's turn to another useful best practice, docstrings.

Getting the most out of docstrings

In this section, we will take a look at how to format docstrings for maximum readability and how to transform them into structured and formatted documentation. We're also going to look at how to make examples in the documentation testable so that the documentation is never out of date.

PEP 257 and docutils

PEP 257 documents the expectations of Python programmers and tools with respect to docstrings. The basic rules are quite simple. These are as follows:

> The documentation is available at `https://www.python.org/dev/peps/pep-0257/`.

- Use triple quotes to delimit the docstring. Triple quotes are how Python expresses the idea of a multiline text string.
- The closing triple quotes should be on a line of their own if your docstring is longer than one line.
- The first line should present a short description of the thing being documented, such as "return the distance between n-points a and b."

After the first line, we can either end the docstring or insert a blank line, followed by a more in-depth description of the documented object, containing descriptions of parameters, attributes, usage semantics examples, and so on (refer to the following screenshot):

```
def docstring_example(foo, bar):
    """Munge foo and bar

    the *foo* parameter should be an instance of :class: 'Thingy', or
    have a method equivalent to :meth: 'Thingy.munge'. It will be
    passed the *bar* argument as its first parameter.

    """
    foo.munge(bar)
```

The reason for this layout is that many tools show the first line of the docstring as a popup, tooltip, or otherwise presented as a quick reference. The text after the blank line is presented when detailed documentation is requested. The docstring processing tools are smart about indentation, so it's safe and encouraged to indent our docstrings, so that they match up with the rest of the code block that they're describing.

Those basic rules are all that are required to make our docstrings interact well with Python's `pydoc` and help tools with IDEs, and so on. But they don't give us any way of creating well-formatted standalone documentation. That's where Sphinx comes into play.

Sphinx

Sphinx is a tool that can process Python source code and standalone documentation files and generate nicely formatted documentation in a number of formats, notably HTML. Sphinx, like other Python documentation tools, recognizes a markup language called `reStructuredText`, which is intentionally readable and informative, even when its markup is presented as plaintext rather than being interpreted.

 `reStructuredText` can be found at the following link: `https://docs.py thon.org/devguide/documenting.html#reStructuredText-primer`.

reStructuredText documents are still readable in a simple text editor, but when we feed them through a tool such as Sphinx they make the end result richer. The reStructuredText syntax is based on the conventions that developed on the internet before actual rich text was widely available in email and real-time chat.

So, for example, words are emphasized by putting an asterisk (`*text*`) at each end and emphasized further by making that into two asterisks (`**text**`). Paragraphs are marked by placing a blank line between them.

There are syntaxes for lists, headings, and so on, all plainly readable in text mode. The syntax is nicely described in the Python developer's guide, but we're going to concentrate on a few bits of markup that do a lot to enhance the documentation for modules and packages. We actually saw one of those bits of markup earlier.

When our docstrings make reference to a local variable, such as a function parameter, that reference should be enclosed in asterisks to emphasize it and make it distinct from the normal text of the documentation. The names of modules, classes, functions, methods, attributes, exceptions, global variables, and constants should all be marked properly, so that Sphinx can cross-reference them and create links to their documentation.

All of these object types share a similar syntax, which is that we put a type identifying keyword between colons, immediately followed by the name of the object in back quotes:

```
the *foo* parameter should be an instance of :class:`Thingy`, or
have a method equivalent to :meth: `Thingy.munge`. It will be
passed the *bar* argument as its first parameter.
```

As you saw in the preceding example with classes and methods, we used the keywords class for `classes` and `meth` for methods. Other keywords available are: `mod` for modules, `func` for functions, `attr` for attributes, `data` for variables, and `const` for constants.

That's enough reStructuresText syntax to make a big difference in the quality of our documentation. So, we're going to leave it there and go on to talk about how to actually use the Sphinx tool. If it's not already installed, we can install it using `pip`, as shown in the following command:

```
(sphinx) $ python3 -m pip install sphinx
```

Sphinx can do a lot more, so it's worth working through the tutorial on https://www.sphinx-doc.org/en/stable/tutorial.html. It's quite nice.

For our own purposes though, all we're interested in is turning docstrings into HTML. So, we'll work through that process in the next sub-section.

Turning docstrings into HTML

We're going to generate HTML documentation for our example package, which is just a docstring example. We start by going to the directory that contains our package directory. Once there, we run `sphinx-quickstart` to set things up.

```
(sphinx) $ ls
bin   include  lib   lib64  pip-selfcheck.json  pyvenv.cfg  refs.py  src
(sphinx) $ cd src
(sphinx) $ ls
example
(sphinx) $ ls example/
__init__.py  refs.py
(sphinx) $ sphinx-quickstart
Welcome to the Sphinx 1.4.8 quickstart utility.

Please enter values for the following settings (just press Enter to
accept a default value, if one is given in brackets).

Enter the root path for documentation. _
```

The first thing that `sphinx-quickstart` asks is what the root path for the documentation should be. I find that it works well to use a folder called `docs` for this, so I suggest typing in `docs` for the root path:

```
Enter the root path for documentation.
> Root path for the documentation [.]: docs

You have two options for placing the build directory for Sphinx output.
Either, you use a directory "_build" within the root path, or you separate
"source" and "build" directories within the root path.
> Separate source and build directories (y/n) [n]:

Inside the root directory, two more directories will be created; "_templates"
for custom HTML templates and "_static" for custom stylesheets and other static
files. You can enter another prefix (such as ".") to replace the underscore.
> Name prefix for templates and static dir [_]:

The project name will occur in several places in the built documentation.
> Project name: Stuff
> Author name(s): Daniel Arbuckle
```

The `sphinx-quickstart` command will ask several more questions, which we can answer as we like, and then eventually it will ask if we want to enable the autodoc plugin; we will enable it by entering yes (y):

```
Sphinx has the notion of a "version" and a "release" for the
software. Each version can have multiple releases. For example, for
Python the version is something like 2.5 or 3.0, while the release is
something like 2.5.1 or 3.0a1.  If you don't need this dual structure,
just set both to the same value.
> Project version: 0.1
> Project release [0.1]:

If the documents are to be written in a language other than English,
you can select a language here by its language code. Sphinx will then
translate text that it generates into that language.

For a list of supported codes, see
http://sphinx-doc.org/config.html#confval-language.
> Project language [en]:

The file name suffix for source files. Commonly, this is either ".txt"
or ".rst".  Only files with this suffix are considered documents.
> Source file suffix [.rst]:

One document is special in that it is considered the top node of the
"contents tree", that is, it is the root of the hierarchical structure
of the documents. Normally, this is "index", but if your "index"
document is a custom template, you can also set this to another filename.
> Name of your master document (without suffix) [index]:

Sphinx can also add configuration for epub output:
> Do you want to use the epub builder (y/n) [n]:

Please indicate if you want to use one of the following Sphinx extensions:
> autodoc: automatically insert docstrings from modules (y/n) [n]: y
```

The rest of the questions are not so important for our purposes. After answering all the questions, the `sphinx-quickstart` command is completed as shown in the following screenshot:

```
Please indicate if you want to use one of the following Sphinx extensions:
> autodoc: automatically insert docstrings from modules (y/n) [n]: y
> doctest: automatically test code snippets in doctest blocks (y/n) [n]:
> intersphinx: link between Sphinx documentation of different projects (y/n) [n]:
> todo: write "todo" entries that can be shown or hidden on build (y/n) [n]:
> coverage: checks for documentation coverage (y/n) [n]:
> imgmath: include math, rendered as PNG or SVG images (y/n) [n]:
> mathjax: include math, rendered in the browser by MathJax (y/n) [n]:
> ifconfig: conditional inclusion of content based on config values (y/n) [n]:
> viewcode: include links to the source code of documented Python objects (y/n) [n]:
> githubpages: create .nojekyll file to publish the document on GitHub pages (y/n) [n]:

A Makefile and a Windows command file can be generated for you so that you
only have to run e.g. `make html' instead of invoking sphinx-build
directly.
> Create Makefile? (y/n) [y]:
> Create Windows command file? (y/n) [y]:

Creating file docs/conf.py.
Creating file docs/index.rst.
Creating file docs/Makefile.
Creating file docs/make.bat.

Finished: An initial directory structure has been created.

You should now populate your master file docs/index.rst and create other documentation
source files. Use the Makefile to build the docs, like so:
    make builder
where "builder" is one of the supported builders, e.g. html, latex or linkcheck.

(sphinx) $ cd doc
bash: cd: doc: No such file or directory
(sphinx) $ cd docs
(sphinx) $ ls
Makefile   _build   _static   _templates   conf.py   index.rst   make.bat
(sphinx) $ emacs conf.py
```

Once `sphinx-quickstart` is completed, we'll want to run `sphinx-apidoc -o` with our directory to automatically generate Sphinx or Sphinx source files describing our package:

```
(sphinx) $ cd ..
(sphinx) $ ls
docs  example
(sphinx) $ sphinx-apidoc -o docs/ example/
Creating file docs/example.rst.
Creating file docs/modules.rst.
(sphinx) $ cd docs
(sphinx) $ make html
sphinx-build -b html -d _build/doctrees   . _build/html
Running Sphinx v1.4.8
making output directory...
loading pickled environment... not yet created
building [mo]: targets for 0 po files that are out of date
building [html]: targets for 3 source files that are out of date
updating environment: 3 added, 0 changed, 0 removed
reading sources... [100%] modules
looking for now-outdated files... none found
pickling environment... done
checking consistency... /home/djarb/tmp/sphinx/src/docs/modules.rst:: WARNING: document isn't included in any toctree
done
preparing documents... done
writing output... [100%] modules
generating indices... genindex py-modindex
writing additional pages... search
copying static files... done
copying extra files... done
dumping search index in English (code: en) ... done
dumping object inventory... done
build succeeded, 1 warning.

Build finished. The HTML pages are in  build/html.
```

Our docstrings are extracted and incorporated into these source files.

Finally, when we want to generate the HTML we can construct it by running `make html` from the command line. Sphinx will translate its source files, including the ones automatically generated by `sphinx-apidoc` into HTML and store the result in the build directory that we specified when we were going through the `sphinx-quickstart` questions.

If we edit our source code and want to update the HTML documentation, we can usually do it simply by running the following command again:

```
(sphinx) $ make html
```

If we've made major changes to the package structure, we'll need to run the `sphinx-apidoc` command again as well:

```
(sphinx) $ sphinx-apidoc -o docs/ example/
```

So, Sphinx can be used as a documentation compiler, which turns our docstrings source code into HTML-compiled code.

Using doctest to test documentation examples

Including examples of use in our docstrings is common, but if we're not careful, those examples can get left behind when the code changes, and the wrong documentation is worse than no documentation. Fortunately, we have a tool that can check whether the documentation agrees with the code by running the examples from our documentation and seeing what happens. That tool is called **doctest**.

To enable doctest to recognize our examples as things it can test, all we have to do is include the Python interactive shell prompt into our example. In the simplest and most common case, that just means putting a >>> symbol in front of each statement, as shown in the following screenshot. For multi-line statements, we prefix the continuation line with a . . . symbol:

```python
def testable(message):
    """A function with testable documentation


    >>> testable('Hello World')
    'Hello World'

    >>> for x in range(5):
    ...     print(x)
    0
    1
    2
    3
    4

    """
    return message
```

After each statement, we should write down the expected result of the statement, written the same way the interactive shell would write it. In other words, if we copy and paste directly from the interactive shell, we've created an example that doctest can recognize. So, writing doctest is pretty straightforward.

There's a decent chance of writing a doctest into our docstrings, even if we didn't know the doctest tool exists. As an added bonus, Sphinx recognizes doctest and formats it appropriately too. So, if we're going to include code examples in our docstrings, the way to do it is explained in the following section.

Testing examples using doctest

To test the code example using doctest, we just need to run the following command:

```
$ python3 -m doctest example.py -v
```

We will get the following output:

```
$ python3 -m doctest example.py -v
Trying:
    testable('Hello World')
Expecting:
    'Hello World'
ok
Trying:
    for x in range(5):
        print(x)
Expecting:
    0
    1
    2
    3
    4
ok
1 items had no tests:
    example
1 items passed all tests:
    2 tests in example.testable
2 tests in 2 items.
2 passed and 0 failed.
Test passed.
```

Having doctest run all the examples in a file and report back whether they worked is easy. We just run the doctest utility from the command line and tell it which files we were interested in. The -v option in the command makes it pull out extra information, which isn't necessary, but often is helpful.

All we see in the preceding example is a lack of error messages rather than any confirmation that everything worked or is tested.

There are other ways of running doctests including a Sphinx plugin that sphinx-quickstart asks us whether we want. It's also possible to integrate doctests into a test suite for Python's standard unit test library, or to use an integrated test runner called nos to find an excuse to execute them; doctests directly will do for our purposes in such cases, though.

What it means when a code example fails

Now, what happens if a doctest fails, but after looking at it we see that the documentation and example are actually correct? Well, that means our code is incorrect. Believe it or not, this is a very good thing. I don't mean that having an error is a good thing, but that error was there whether we found it or not. Finding it and having a test on hand that will let us check whether we've succeeded in fixing it, though, is definitely good.

So, doctest ties our code and documentation together, so that they stay synchronized and serve to double-check each other. That's a very useful docstring trick.

Summary

In this chapter, you learned about writing readable code, version control to keep track of our code, and about the venv tool and the isolated virtual environments it creates. You learned how to format our docstrings to take advantage of automated tools, such as IDEs and the Sphinx documentation compiler. You also learned about writing examples into our documentation and how to use the doctest tool to check whether the examples and code are synchronized

In the next chapter, you'll get to learn how to turn a package into a program that can be run from the command line.

5
Making a Command-Line Utility

In the previous chapter, we visited some best practices that would help us in the long run when using Python. In this chapter, we're going to see how to make Python command-line programs and some features that make such programs easier and more useful. We're going to see how to create an entry point for code execution in a package and see how to run the package as a program.

We're also going to see how to make the program read data from its command line and how to easily handle reading data from our program's command-line arguments. We'll also look at how to actually run other programs from inside our code.

In this chapter, we will cover the following topics:

- Making a package executable via Python `-m`
- Handling command-line argument with `argparse`
- Python tools to interact with the user
- Executing other programs with subprocess
- Using shell script or batch files to run our programs

Making a package executable via Python -m

In the previous chapter, we ran command-line tools, such as doctest and venv, by typing in the python3 -m command followed by the name of the tool we wanted it to run:

```
devesh@devesh-VirtualBox:~$ python3 -m venv
usage: venv [-h] [--system-site-packages] [--symlinks | --copies] [--clear]
            [--upgrade] [--without-pip]
            ENV_DIR [ENV_DIR ...]
venv: error: the following arguments are required: ENV_DIR
devesh@devesh-VirtualBox:~$
```

What were we actually asking Python to do when we did that?

The -m command-line switch for Python tells it to run a module. It uses the same mechanism to find the module that it would if we'd used an import statement with the module's name and then it executes it.

However, venv isn't a module, it's a package. So, what's happening when we use python -m venv? We gave Python a package name, but we didn't give it a module name inside the package that it should run. When that happens, Python looks for a module named __main__ in the package and runs that:

```
devesh@devesh-VirtualBox:~$ python3 -m venv.__main__
usage: venv [-h] [--system-site-packages] [--symlinks | --copies] [--clear]
            [--upgrade] [--without-pip]
            ENV_DIR [ENV_DIR ...]
venv: error: the following arguments are required: ENV_DIR
devesh@devesh-VirtualBox:~$
```

So, python -m venv means the same thing as python -m venv.__main__.

Any module that's meant to contain a program's entry point has a problem because simply importing the module will run the code too. This can be annoying or troublesome at the best of times, but it becomes unacceptable when we're using tools, such as Sphinx or doctest, that need to import modules in order to do their jobs, but which really shouldn't actually run the module code as a program.

Fortunately, there's an easy fix because the Python interpreter itself knows which module it was told to start running and marks it as such. All modules are automatically given a variable called __name__, which contains the module's name. All modules, that is, except for the program entry point.

The program entry point is always given the name __main__, even if its filename is something entirely different:

```
def main_function():
    print("Here we go!")

if __name__ == '__main__':
    main_function()
```

So, we can check whether our code was the program entry point by checking this, __name__ == '__main__'. If our code was indeed the program entry point, then we should run the program, as in the example above. If it isn't, we would import it normally as code and should not run the program as main code.

This distinguishes between importing of the __main__ module of the package and running it. Because when we import it, the name variable contains the package name __main__, not just __main__. In the upcoming sections in this chapter, we're going to work through the process of building a complete utility program called **Pipeline**.

Pipeline program

Pipeline will be a text-mode program that can be configured to run a sequence of other programs and feed data from each program into the next. In each section, we'll apply what we talked about developing Pipeline further.

So far, what we talked about in this chapter is how to make the program able to be run from python -m, but in the previous chapters, we saw how to create a virtual environment to work in, how to create a package, and how to layout the code in the packages modules for readability.

So, let's put those lessons to use.

Create a folder within the virtual environment to be the package and call it `pipeline`. Inside the `package` folder, place an `__init__.py` file, which can be empty, and a `__main__.py` file:

```
devesh@devesh-VirtualBox:~$ ls pipeline/
__init__.py  __main__.py  __pycache__
```

For now, the contents of the `__main__.py` file can be very simple, as shown in the following screenshot:

```
""" Run a sequence of programs.

Each program (except the first) receives the standard output of the
previous program on its standard input, by default. There are several
alternate ways of passing data between the programs.

"""

def _launch():
    print('Pipeline launched!')

if __name__ == '__main__':
    _launch()
```

The contents of the `__main__.py` file are as follows:

- A docstring for the module
- A function that should be called if the module is the program entry point
- The `if` statement that decides whether or not to call the **launch function**

The launch function doesn't have a docstring, which is allowed because it's marked as non-public by having an underscore as the first letter of its name. The launch function also doesn't do anything interesting yet; it just uses the print function to tell us that it was successfully executed.

Let's run it so we can see for ourselves.

1. Open a command-line window,
2. Go to the virtual environment where we created the package

3. Activate the virtual environment.
4. Then, type the following command:

```
(pipeline) $ python –m pipeline
```

The output is as follows:

```
devesh@devesh-VirtualBox:~$ python3 -m pipeline
Pipeline launched
devesh@devesh-VirtualBox:~$ 
```

We should see the message printed out (as shown in the preceding screenshot) and then the program will end.

Handling command-line arguments with argparse

In this section, we'll see how to make the program read data from its command line, a common feature for programs of all sorts. Most command-line programs and a surprising number of graphical user interface programs as well can be given extra information on the command line, after the command that invokes the program. These extra bits of information are referred to as **arguments** and they are delivered to Python programs as a list of strings. It turns out that there's quite a lot of code involved in turning an argument list into useful information, especially, if we want to make the program as convenient for our users as possible. Fortunately, a lot of that code can be the same from program to program, and the Python standard library's **argparse** module takes care of much of the effort for us.

Creating an ArgumentParser object

The primary component of the `argparse` module is the `ArgumentParser` class. In the minimal case, it only takes three lines of code to use `argparse`. We need to import it, create an argument parser instance, and call that instance's `parse_args()` function:

```
import argparse
parser = argparse.ArgumentParser()
args = parser.parse_args()
```

As usual, with minimal cases that's not very useful. The only arguments that the program will respond to are -h or --help, either of which would print out an automatically generated `how to use this program` message and then exit the program.

The first thing we could do to make the `ArgumentParser` class more useful is to provide a value for the `description` parameter of its constructor, as shown in the following screenshot:

```
import argparse
parser = argparse.ArgumentParser(description="Hello world")
args = parser.parse_args()
```

ArgumentParser's automatically generated help message will explain all the arguments that the program expects, but it doesn't say anything about what the program is actually supposed to do, unless we provide a description ourselves.

The next way we can improve the ArgumentParser's behavior is by telling it the name of the program. If we don't provide a name, it will do its best to make a reasonable guess, but we're better off telling it ourselves. I consider the `python3 -m` command (refer to the following code example) to be the canonical name for my own programs so that's what we'll use in our examples:

```
import argparse
parser = argparse.ArgumentParser(
    prog = 'python -m apdemo',
    description="Hello world"
)
args = parser.parse_args()
```

Setting the name of argument

We set the name of an argument by passing it as a string to the `ArgumentParser` constructor's `prog` parameter. These changes make the help output of the program prettier and more useful, but they don't actually give the program any new capabilities.

We need to start adding argument specifications to the parser, so it can check for them in the argument list.

We do that by calling the `ArgumentParser` instance's `add_argument` method:

```
import argparse
parser = argparse.ArgumentParser(
    prog = 'python -m apdemo',
    description="Hello world"
)
parser.add_argument('-p', '--print', action='store_true', default = False)
args = parser.parse_args()
```

The `argparse` module recognizes two kinds of arguments:

- Optional arguments
- Positional arguments

As the name implies, **optional arguments** are not required, but if the user chooses to include them, they have meaning. **Positional arguments**, on the other hand, are required by default, although we can modify that behavior. Optional arguments have names that start with the – character. They can have more than one alternate name for the same argument. The names are passed as parameters to the `add_argument` method, as in the preceding example, where –p and --print are alternate names for the same optional argument.

There are a lot of ways of configuring an argument when we add it to the parser, which are detailed in the `argparse` documentation in the library reference at `https://docs.python.org/3/`.

For options like our print example though, the important configuration items are `action` and `default`:

- The `action` parameter tells `argparse` what to do when it finds the argument on the command line
- The `default` parameter tells it what to do when it doesn't find the argument on the command line

The `action` parameter can either be a string containing the name of one of the well-known actions, such as `store_true`, or it could be a subclass of the `argparse.action` class:

```
import argparse
parser = argparse.ArgumentParser(
    prog = 'python -m apdemo',
    description="Hello world"
)
parser.add_argument('-p', '--print', action='store_true', default = False)
parser.add_argument('name', nargs='+')
args = parser.parse_args()
```

The `default` parameter can be any arbitrary value, which will be stored as the value of the argument. If it's missing when we actually ask the `parser` to parse out the argument values, the other kind of argument has to have just one name and it can't start with a – character.

By default, these arguments collect one word that isn't part of an optional argument from the command line in the order that they were added to the parser. If we configure the argument using the `nargs` option, we can change the number of words that the argument collects.

nargs

If we set `nargs` to a number, that many words will be collected for the argument. We can also set `nargs` to * to mean any number of words or + to mean at least one word. There are a few other values we could set `nargs` to, but we won't talk about them here in this section.

Let's look back at our Pipeline program. I think we want it to understand two arguments-an optional argument that tells it to keep going, even if one of the programs returns an error code, and a filename, where it should load and store a pipeline configuration:

```
"""Run a sequence of programs.

Each program (except the first) receives the standard output of the
previous program on its standard input, by default. There are several
alternate ways of passing data between the programs.

"""

import argparse

def _launch():
    parser = argparse.ArgumentParser(prog = 'python -m pipeline',
                                     description = __doc__)
    parser.add_argument('-k','--keep-going',
                        action = 'store_true',
                        default = False)

    parser.add_argument('filename')

    args = parser.parse_args()

    print(args.keep_going)
    print(args.filename)

if __name__ == '__main__':
    _launch()
```

After the call to parse parse_args, we have an object named args that contains a keep_going attribute set to either true or false and a filename attribute containing a string.

 Notice that the attribute of the arguments object is keep_going, not keep-going. Python doesn't allow – characters inside of attribute names and argparse is smart enough to fix that for us automatically.

If we wanted to set the name of the argument object attribute manually, we could have passed the name we wanted to the add_argument method as its best parameter.

Python tools to interact with the user

In the previous section, we saw how to get information from the user on the command line, but what do we do when we need a more dynamic form of interaction? So, let's take a look at some of Python's tools for sending information to the user and requesting information from the user.

Python's built-in functions - print and input

The fundamentals of interactivity are simple. We need to be able to tell the user things and we need the user to be able to tell us things. In service of those two goals, Python provides two built-in functions. These are `print` and `input`.

Create a `simple.py` file with the following code:

```
print("Hello World")
name = input("Name: ")
print("Hello", name)
```

The `print` function takes any number of Python objects as parameters and prints them on the screen. The `input` function takes a string prompt as its parameter, prints it out, then reads text until the user hits *Enter*, and returns what the user typed as a string.

Run the following command to see how the `print` and `input` functions work:

```
python3 simple.py
```

That's about as simple as interactivity can get. The following screenshot shows the output of the preceding command:

```
devesh@devesh-VirtualBox:~$ python3 simple.py
Hello World
Name :Devesh
Hello Devesh
```

The `print` and `input` functions can do a lot, but there are a couple of corner cases where they don't work so well.

The getpass package

One of those corner cases I just mentioned is when we want the user to type in a password. If we use the `input` function to read the password, it would be displayed on the screen for anybody to read. The `getpass` package contains a function, also called `getpass`, which works just like `input`, except that it doesn't show the text that the user types.

```
from getpass import getpass
from pprint import pprint

password = getpass('Password: ')
pprint([{1: 2, 3: 4}, {5: 6, 7: list(range(25))}])
```

The other corner case I want to mention is that, although the `print` function can print out any Python object, it doesn't do a good job presenting complex data structures.

The pprint package

The `pprint` function, from the package of the same name, makes complex data structures much more readable. If we want to display a list of dictionaries, `pprint` will do a better job of it than the `print` function would.

Create a `special.py` file with the following code:

```
from getpass import getpass
from pprint import pprint

password = getpass('Password: ')
pprint([{1: 2, 3: 4}, {5: 6, 7: list(range(25))}])
```

Run the following command to execute the `special.py` file:

```
python3 special.py
```

The following screenshot is the output of the preceding command:

```
devesh@devesh-VirtualBox:~$ python3 special.py
Password:
[{1: 2, 3: 4},
 {5: 6,
  7: [0,
      1,
      2,
      3,
      4,
      5,
      6,
      7,
      8,
      9,
      10,
      11,
      12,
      13,
      14,
      15,
      16,
      17,
      18,
      19,
      20,
      21,
      22,
      23,
      24]}]
devesh@devesh-VirtualBox:~$
```

Between these four functions - `print`, `input`, `getpass`, and `pprint` - there's a wide range of user interfaces we could make, but they are pretty basic tools. We'd be reinventing a lot of wheels and wasting time. Fortunately, thanks to Python's *batteries included* philosophy, we don't have to do that. Instead, we'll use the `cmd` package of the standard libraries to quickly build our user interface.

The cmd class

All we have to do is inherit from the `cmd` class and define the methods that implement commands the user can type.

Create a `usecmd.py` file with the following code:

```
import cmd

class Interface(cmd.Cmd):
    prompt = 'Command: '

    def do_foo(self, arg):
        print(arg)

interface = Interface()
interface.cmdloop()
```

We'll set the prompt attribute to a string that will be used to prompt the user for a command. Run the following command to execute the `usecmd.py` file:

```
$ python3 usecmd.py
```

The output of the preceding command is as follows:

```
devesh@devesh-VirtualBox:~$ python3 usecmd.py
Command : help

Documented commands (type help <topic>):
========================================
help

Undocumented commands:
======================
foo

Command :
```

Next, we'll create an instance of our `Interface` class (shown in the following screenshot) and call it the `cmdloop` method. Presto! Instant interface:

```
Command: quit
*** Unknown syntax: quit
Command: Traceback (most recent call last):
  File "usecmd.py", line 10, in <module>
    interface.cmdloop()
  File "/usr/lib64/python3.5/cmd.py", line 126, in cmdloop
    line = input(self.prompt)
KeyboardInterrupt
$
```

In this example, we see that the `cmd` class takes care of displaying props, reading and commands, and invoking the correct methods, but that's all it does. We still need the `print` function if we want to display data from inside of a command handler method.

The `cmd` class isn't exclusive. It does a lot of work for us, but we could still use the `print` and `input` functions directly, if we need to. That's very nearly everything there is to say about text mode interactivity in Python, at least if we want our programs to be portable across platforms.

The Pipeline user interface

There's another standard library module called `curses`, which enables much more sophisticated text load operations; however, as the `curses` module is not portable to Windows, we're not going to go into detail in this chapter.

Instead, let's look at defining the user interface for our **Pipeline** program:

```python
class TextInterface(cmd.Cmd):
    """Text-based interface for Pipeline"""

    def __init__(self, keep_going, filename):
        super().__init__(completekey = 'tab')
        self.keep_going = keep_going
        self.path = Path(filename)
        self.prompt = 'Pipeline> '

        try:
            with self.path.open('rb') as f:
                self.steps = pickle.load(f)
        except FileNotFoundError:
            self.steps = []

    def do_save(self, arg):
        """Save the pipeline"""
        if not self.path.parent.exists():
            self.path.parent.mkdir(parents = True)

        with self.path.open('wb') as f:
            pickle.dump(self.steps, f)

    def do_quit(self, arg):
        """Exit Pipeline"""
        sys.exit(0)

    def do_exec(self, arg):
        """Append a program invocation to the pipeline"""
```

```python
    """Run a sequence of programs.

    Each program (except the first) receives the standard output of the
    previous program on its statndard input, by default. There are
    several alternate ways of passing data between the programs.

    """

import argparse

from pipeline.interface import TextInterface

def _launch():
    parser = argparse.ArgumentParser(prog = 'python -m pipeline',
                                     description = __doc__)
    parser.add_argument('-k','--keep-going',
                        action = 'store_true'
                        default = False)

    parser.add_argument('filename')

    args = parser.parse_args()

    iface = TextInterface(args.keep_going, args.filename)
    iface.cmdloop()

if __name__ == '__main__':
    _launch()
```

Now it seems like we'd want to be able to add programs to Pipeline and manipulate the data passing between the programs in various ways:

```
(pipeline) $ python3 -m pipeline
usage: python -m pipeline [-h] [-k] filename
python -m pipeline: error: the following arguments are required: filename
(pipeline) $ python3 -m pipeline example
```

We'll also want to be able to save the pipeline when we're happy with it and to be able to actually run it. Finally, we'll want to be able to quit the program using the quit command.

A help command would also be helpful, but luckily, the cmd class will provide that automatically using the docstrings for the command handler functions:

```
Pipeline> help

Documented commands (type help <topic>):
========================================
args   exec   help   inject   quit   run   save   store

Pipeline> help args
Use the last output as arguments instead of input
Pipeline> quit
(pipeline) $
```

We're just going to stub in the command handlers here because we're focusing on the interface implementation for now. So, there we have a pretty decent user interface with very little work on our part. That wraps up our look at text-mode interaction here. Let's now focus on some of our options around program control.

Executing other programs with subprocess

In this section, you will learn how to execute and control other programs from within our own, allowing us to create the heart of our example program. This ability is often useful for all sorts of system automation tasks. Create an `echo.py` file with the following content:

```python
while True:
    x = input()
    print('echoed:', x)
```

Making other programs run used to be something of a mess. There were different mechanisms that worked on different platforms, there were mechanisms that were convenient and there were different mechanisms that were secure. Fortunately, all that changed since Python version 2.4 with the introduction of the `subprocess` module, which abstracts away the differences between platforms and makes some more secure paradigms easy to use.

Subprocess and its variants

There are six objects in the `subprocess` package that are of particular interest. Three of them are the `call`, `check_call`, and `check_output` functions, which are three variants on the same basic idea:

```python
from subprocess import call, check_call, check_output
```

These three objects run a program, wait for it to terminate, and then tell us something about what the program did:

- The `call` function returns the program's exit code, which is an integer that has a program-defined meaning, which is usually used to know whether the program has succeeded or failed.
- The `check_call` function raises an exception if the program's exit code is non-zero, which, by convention, means that it exited with an error.
- The `check_output` function returns whatever text the program printed and raises an exception if the program exited with a non-zero exit code. The raised exception has an attribute called `output` that contains the text output of the program. So, even if the program exited with an error code, we could still get the output if we want it.

The run function is similar to the `call` function we were looking at just a moment ago:

```
from subprocess import run
```

In fact, the run function is capable of doing anything that anyone would do, in combination. However it is not necessarily possible to use it in other projects, at least not yet.

The three call functions and the run function are invoked in largely the same way. Each of them is passed as a list containing the program name and its arguments. We see the output of this `'ls'`, `'-l'` function on the screen that wasn't from the call because `'ls'`, `'-l'` prints something out when it runs.

Type the following statement:

```
call(['ls', '-l', '/dev/null'])
```

The following is the output of the preceding statement:

```
>>> call(['ls', '-l', '/dev/null'])
crw-rw-rw- 1 root root 1, 3 Jun 20 17:52 /dev/null
0
>>>
```

The exit code returned 0, though. So that becomes your call. If you wanted to take that printout from the `'ls'` program and use it in our program, we need to capture it.

The `check_output` function has a noteworthy keyword-only parameter called `universal_newlines`, which defaults to `False`. If we set `universal_newlines` to `True`, the text output of the program is decoded into unicode characters, using the system's default text codec, and the newline characters are normalized.

If we leave `universal_newlines` at its default value of `False`, the program output is returned as bytes and it's up to us to do any decoding and to deal with whatever sequence of characters the current system considers to be a newline character:

```
lines = check_output(['ls', '-l', '/dev/'], universal_newlines =
True).split('\n')
```

Now type the following and press *Enter*:

```
lines
```

In this code example, we did set `universal_newlines` to `True` and then split it at `\n`, which is the standard newline character, and that gave us back a list of the lines that are output from the program:

```
>>> lines = check_output(['ls', '-l', '/dev/'], universal_newlines = True).split("\n")
>>> lines
['total 0', 'crw-------  1 root root    10, 235 Jun 20 17:52 autofs', 'drwxr-xr-x  2 root root         620 Jun 20 17:52 block', 'drw
xr-xr-x  2 root root       80 Jun 20 17:52 bsg', 'crw-rw----  1 root disk    10, 234 Jun 21 00:27 btrfs-control', 'drwxr-xr-x  3
root root       60 Jun 20 17:52 bus', 'lrwxrwxrwx  1 root root         3 Jun 20 17:52 cdrom -> sr0', 'drwxr-xr-x  2 root root
3600 Jun 21 00:27 char', 'crw-------  1 root root     5,   1 Jun 20 17:53 console', 'lrwxrwxrwx  1 root root          11 Jun 20
17:52 core -> /proc/kcore', 'drwxr-xr-x  2 root root       60 Jun 20 17:52 cpu', 'crw-------  1 root root    10,  59 Jun 20 17:5
2 cpu_dma_latency', 'crw-------  1 root root    10, 203 Jun 20 17:52 cuse', 'drwxr-xr-x  5 root root         100 Jun 20 17:52 disk',
'drwxr-xr-x  2 root root       80 Jun 20 17:52 drl', 'lrwxrwxrwx  1 root root         3 Jun 20 17:52 dvd -> sr0', 'crw-------
1 root root    10,  61 Jun 20 17:53 ecryptfs', 'crw-rw----  1 root video    29,   0 Jun 20 17:53 fb0', 'lrwxrwxrwx  1 root root
13 Jun 20 17:52 fd -> /proc/self/fd', 'crw-rw-rw-  1 root root     1,   7 Jun 20 17:52 full', 'crw-rw-rw-  1 root root     10,
229 Jun 21 00:25 fuse', 'crw-------  1 root root   248,   0 Jun 20 17:52 hidraw0', 'crw-------  1 root root    10, 228 Jun 20 17:52
hpet', 'drwxr-xr-x  2 root root       0 Jun 20 17:52 hugepages', 'crw-------  1 root root    10, 183 Jun 20 17:53 hwrng', 'crw-
-------  1 root root    89,   0 Jun 20 17:53 i2c-0', 'lrwxrwxrwx  1 root root          25 Jun 20 17:52 initctl -> /run/systemd/initct
l/fifo', 'drwxr-xr-x  4 root root       60 Jun 20 17:52 lightnvm', 'lrwxrwxrwx  1 root root          28 Jun 20 17:52 log -> /run/systemd/journal/dev
-log', 'brw-rw----  1 root disk     7,   0 Jun 20 17:52 loop0', 'brw-rw----  1 root disk     7,   1 Jun 20 17:52 loop1', 'brw-rw--
--  1 root disk     7,   2 Jun 20 17:52 loop2', 'brw-rw----  1 root disk     7,   3 Jun 20 17:52 loop3', 'brw-rw----  1 root disk
7,   4 Jun 20 17:52 loop4', 'brw-rw----  1 root disk     7,   5 Jun 20 17:52 loop5', 'brw-rw----  1 root disk     7,   6 Jun 20
17:52 loop6', 'brw-rw----  1 root disk     7,   7 Jun 20 17:52 loop7', 'crw-rw----  1 root disk    10, 237 Jun 21 00:25 loop-contro
l', 'drwxr-xr-x  2 root root       60 Jun 20 17:53 mapper', 'crw-------  1 root root    10, 227 Jun 20 17:53 mcelog', 'crw-r-----
1 root kmem     1,   1 Jun 20 17:52 mem', 'crw-------  1 root root    10,  56 Jun 20 17:53 memory_bandwidth', 'drwxrwxrwt  2 root
root       40 Jun 20 17:52 mqueue', 'drwxr-xr-x  2 root root       60 Jun 20 17:52 net', 'crw-------  1 root root    10,  58
Jun 20 17:53 network_latency', 'crw-------  1 root root    10,  57 Jun 20 17:53 network_throughput', 'crw-rw-rw-  1 root root     1
,   3 Jun 20 17:52 null', 'crw-r-----  1 root kmem     1,   4 Jun 20 17:52 port', 'crw-------  1 root root   108,   0 Jun 20 17:53
ppp', 'crw-------  1 root root    10,   1 Jun 20 17:53 psaux', 'crw-rw-rw-  1 root tty      5,   2 Jun 21 16:22 ptmx', 'drwxr-xr-x
2 root root       0 Jun 20 17:52 pts', 'brw-rw----  1 root disk     1,   0 Jun 20 17:52 ram0', 'brw-rw----  1 root disk     1,
1 Jun 20 17:52 ram1', 'brw-rw----  1 root disk     1,  10 Jun 20 17:52 ram10', 'brw-rw----  1 root disk     1,  11 Jun 20 17:52
ram11', 'brw-rw----  1 root disk     1,  12 Jun 20 17:52 ram12', 'brw-rw----  1 root disk     1,  13 Jun 20 17:52 ram13', 'brw-rw-
---  1 root disk     1,  14 Jun 20 17:52 ram14', 'brw-rw----  1 root disk     1,  15 Jun 20 17:52 ram15', 'brw-rw----  1 root disk
1,   2 Jun 20 17:52 ram2', 'brw-rw----  1 root disk     1,   3 Jun 20 17:52 ram3', 'brw-rw----  1 root disk     1,   4 Jun 20 1
7:52 ram4', 'brw-rw----  1 root disk     1,   5 Jun 20 17:52 ram5', 'brw-rw----  1 root disk     1,   6 Jun 20 17:52 ram6', 'brw-rw
----  1 root disk     1,   7 Jun 20 17:52 ram7', 'brw-rw----  1 root disk     1,   8 Jun 20 17:52 ram8', 'brw-rw----  1 root disk
1,   9 Jun 20 17:52 ram9', 'brw-rw----  1 root disk     1,   2 Jun 20 17:52 random', 'crw-rw-r--+ 1 root netdev    10,  62 Jun 20
17:53 rfkill', 'lrwxrwxrwx  1 root root         4 Jun 20 17:52 rtc -> rtc0', 'crw-------  1 root root   251,   0 Jun 20 17:52 rtc
0', 'brw-rw----  1 root disk     8,   0 Jun 20 17:52 sda', 'brw-rw----  1 root disk     8,   1 Jun 20 17:52 sda1', 'brw-rw----  1 r
oot disk     8,   2 Jun 20 17:52 sda2', 'brw-rw----  1 root disk     8,   5 Jun 20 17:52 sda5', 'crw-rw----+ 1 root cdrom    21,
0 Jun 20 17:52 sg0', 'crw-rw----  1 root disk    21,   1 Jun 20 17:52 sg1', 'drwxrwxrwt  2 root root         200 Jun 20 17:56 shm',
'crw-------  1 root root    10, 231 Jun 20 17:53 snapshot', 'drwxr-xr-x  3 root root         180 Jun 20 17:53 snd', 'brw-rw----+ 1 r
oot cdrom    11,   0 Jun 20 17:52 sr0', 'lrwxrwxrwx  1 root root          15 Jun 20 17:52 stderr -> /proc/self/fd/2', 'lrwxrwxrwx  1
root root          15 Jun 20 17:52 stdin -> /proc/self/fd/0', 'lrwxrwxrwx  1 root root          15 Jun 20 17:52 stdout -> /proc/self/
fd/1', 'crw-rw-rw-  1 root tty      5,   0 Jun 21 13:52 tty', 'crw-w----  1 root tty      4,   0 Jun 20 17:53 tty0', 'crw-w----
1 root tty      4,   1 Jun 20 17:53 tty1', 'crw-w----  1 root tty      4,  10 Jun 20 17:53 tty10', 'crw-w----  1 root tty      4
, 11 Jun 20 17:53 tty11', 'crw-w----  1 root tty      4,  12 Jun 20 17:53 tty12', 'crw-w----  1 root tty      4,  13 Jun 20 17:5
3 tty13', 'crw-w----  1 root tty      4,  14 Jun 20 17:53 tty14', 'crw-w----  1 root tty      4,  15 Jun 20 17:53 tty15', 'crw-w-
----  1 root tty      4,  16 Jun 20 17:53 tty16', 'crw-w----  1 root tty      4,  17 Jun 20 17:53 tty17', 'crw-w----  1 root tty
4,  18 Jun 20 17:53 tty18', 'crw-w----  1 root tty      4,  19 Jun 20 17:53 tty19', 'crw-w----  1 root tty      4,   2 Jun
```

If we want to get fancier with our running of other programs, we'll want to use instances of the `Popen` class-the fourth interesting thing in the `subprocess` package and which allows us a great deal of flexibility and control over the execution of other programs.

Using the Popen subprocess

At the cost of a bit more complexity, the Popen constructor accepts the same list of program and command-line arguments that the call functions do and a very large number of optional keyword arguments, including universal_newlines.

We're going to focus on a particular use of the Popen constructor that is useful, but goes beyond what we can achieve using one of the call functions. We're going to see how to run a program in the background while our own code is also running, and send and receive data between the two programs.

The PIPE constant

To manage that, we're going to need the last of our six interesting things in the subprocess package-the PIPE constant. The PIPE constant is used in conjunction with the stdin, stdout, or stderr keyword parameters of the Popen constructor:

```
p = Popen(['python3', 'echo.py'], stdin = PIPE, stout = PIPE, bufsize = 0)
```

These parameters represent the other program's textual input, output, and error reporting. Any of them that we set to PIPE are redirected to our program. In the preceding example, we're redirecting the program's inputs and output to ourselves, which gives us a bi-directional data channel with the other programs.

Now you see, we are interacting programmatically with the code on screen that was at the beginning of this example. However, since it sets in a loop, inputs, and then outputs, accord. Also, whenever there is input, once we have PIPE set up, we could send data to the other program by calling the write method on the Popen object's stdin attribute:

```
>>> p.stdin.write(b'Hello\n')
6
>>> p.stdin.flush()
>>> p.stdout.flush()
>>> p.stdout.readline()
b'echoed: Hello\n'
>>>
```

We can read data by calling the `read` method or its relatives on the Popen object's `stdout` attribute, as shown in the preceding example code.

In spite of disabling buffering with the `bufsize = 0` parameter to the `Popen` constructor, it's usually a good idea to call the `flush` method on `stdin` after writing to it and on `stdout` before reading from it. We can keep on sending and receiving data for as long as both programs are running. However, if the time comes when we're done interacting and just want to wait for the other program to terminate, we can call the Popen object's `wait` method to do that.

The wait method

The `wait` method will return the exit code of the other program once it's done running. A lot of the complexity of working with `PIPE`, `stdin`, and `stdout` is wrapped up in the `Popen` class's `communicate` method, which accepts the input as a parameter and returns the output:

```
>>> p.stdin.write(b'Goodbye\n')
8
>>> p.stdin.flush()
>>> p.stdout.flush()
>>> p.stdout.readline()
b'echoed: Goodbye\n'
>>> exit_code = p.wait()
```

Communication is simple, but somewhat limited because it can only be called once for each `Popen` object and doesn't return until the other program finishes. This isn't any good for two programs that need to talk back and forth to each other, but it should be just perfect for our pipeline program, where each program receives the output of the previous program as its input.

Finishing up our code example

We're going to create a bunch of classes to represent the different kinds of steps in the pipeline and integrate those classes into the interface as well. Once we've done that, the program is functional, although there's plenty of room for improvement.

Our particular interest is the `ExecStep` class on the top right-hand side of the following screenshot, which uses `Popen` to actually execute a program and break free of the output.

```
"""Encapsulates single steps of the pipeline           class ExecStep(Step):
                                                            """Represents the execution of a program as a pipelin
Each step type is represented by a subclass of Step, which is
instantiated by the interface.                              def __init__(self.args):
                                                                """Collect the command line for the executed prog
"""                                                             self.args = args

from subprocess import Popen, PIPE                           def run(self, data, args):
from datetime import datetime                                   """Run the program with the given input and argum
from datetime.now()                                             p = Popen(self.args + args,
                                                                          stdin=PIPE,
class Step:                                                               stdout=PIPE,
    """An abstract representation of a single pipeline                    bufsize=0,
    step"""                                                              universal_newlines=True)
                                                                out, err = p.communicate(data)
    def run(self, data, args):                                  return out, []
        """Execute the step
                                                        class ArgsStep(Step):
        The parameters are string data to feed into the pipeline    """Split the output of the prior step into arguments"
        additional arguments to pass to the program.
                                                            def __init__(self, seperator = None):
        The return value is a 2-tuple containing string data to         """Collect the seperator pattern to use for split
        the next program, and a list of command line are pass to the    self.separator = seperator
        next program.
                                                            def run(self, data, args):
        For steps that do not represent execution of a program          """Perform the split and return the results as"""
        warnings are analogous.                                 return '', args + data.split(self.seperator)

        """                                             class StoreStep(Step):
                                                            """Redirect the output of the prior step into a file"
        return '', []
```

We've got our example program working now, so we're going to move on to the last section in this chapter.

Setting up a shell script or batch file to launch the program

In this section, we're going to wrap up this chapter's example program by making it simple to launch. We can run our program using `python -m` as long as it's installed in the system `PYTHONPATH` or we've activated the virtual environment containing it, as shown here:

```
#!/bin/sh
cd /path/to/pipeline/venv
source bin/activate
python -m pipeline list
```

```
@echo off
cd \path\to\piplene\venv
Scripts\activate
python -m pipeline list
```

Creating launches for our program

Once the program is solid, we really just want to be able to type its name or double-click on it and have it run. One convenient way to do that is to use a shell script or a batch file:

- On Unix-style operating systems including macOS, a shell script is a text file that starts with `#bang/bin/sh` and has been marked as executable
- On Windows, a batch file is a file whose name ends in `.bat`

Both shell scripts and batch files are text files containing a sequence of command-line commands, one on each line. When we type the name of the script or batch file, those commands are executed one after the other, as if we type them all into the command line.

Similarly, if we trigger the script or batch file through a graphical user interface, the commands are still executed as if we typed them into a command line one by one. Consider this example:

```
$ pipeline.sh
Pipeline> help

Documented commands (type help <topic>):
========================================
args   exec   help   inject   quit   run   save   store

Pipeline> quit
$
```

For our purposes here, this means that we can put whatever sequence of commands necessary to launch a program into a shell script or a batch file. After that, we could treat that script as if it were the program itself. That's all there is to the simple case.

Shell scripts are capable of representing a lot more complexity, but Python is a better tool for that. So, the simple case, here, is all we really need.

Summary

In the earlier sections of the chapter, you learned about how to make our Python packages into programs, get data from the command line, interact with the user, and run other programs as subprocesses. We saw how to make our Python programs as simple to watch as any other program from the GUI or the command line. We constructed a user interface for our Pipeline program and learned about several of Python's text mode tools along the way.

In the next chapter, we'll look at how to use parallel processing to take advantage of computers with multiple processors or cores.

6
Parallel Processing

In the previous chapter, we created a text mode utility program and you learned about several of Python's built-in packages. In this chapter, we're going to see how to use both the high-level `concurrent.futures` package and the lower-level multiprocessing package to help us write parallel programs. Both are part of the Python standard library.

We will cover the following two topics in detail:

- Using the `concurrent.futures` package
- Using multiprocessing packages

Using the concurrent.futures package

In this section, we're focusing on `concurrent.futures`, the more abstract and easier to use of the two packages mentioned earlier. Our focus will be on the four main operations in `concurrent.futures`. We will then move on to the usage of future objects and end with the implications of the mechanism of data transfer between processes.

Some programs are what we call CPU-bound, which means that the primary factor which determines how long the program takes to complete its tasks is how fast the computer can run through its instructions. Interestingly, most programs that we use on a daily basis are not CPU-bound. However, for those that are, we can often speed them up by breaking them into separate processes.

This difference can be illustrated as follows:

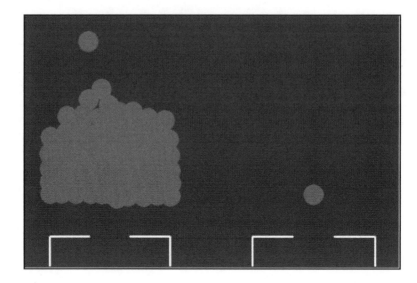

In the preceding figure, on the left-hand side, we have a CPU-bound program. It has many things to do, represented by circles and the speed of execution depends on how quickly the CPU can process. On the right-hand side, we have a program that is not CPU-bound, which means, most of the time, it is waiting for the execution.

The processes can run simultaneously on different CPU cores or even on completely separate CPUs. This has the net effect of increasing the number of program instructors executed per second, which means that CPU-bound programs run faster than the programs that are not CPU-bound.

In some programming languages, we can see the same benefit by running multiple threads for a single program. However, as I mentioned earlier, most programs are not CPU-bound, so the creators of Python have chosen to optimize Python's threading system for the common case, which has the side effect of making Python threads not very useful for improving the speed of CPU-bound programs.

 Besides, it's easier for the operating system to optimize the execution of multiple processes than multiple threads within a process. So, even if threading were a viable option, multiple processes would be a better choice for a CPU-bound program.

We already saw one very low-level approach to launching a process and communicating with it in our discussion of the subprocess module (refer to the *Executing other programs with subprocess* section in Chapter 5, *Making a Command-Line Utility*). However, for cases where the reason we want to do that is because our program is broken up into a bunch of cooperative processes that work together, Python provides us with a couple of higher-level toolkits that make things easier. The more abstract of Python's parallel processing toolkits is called concurrent.futures.

The concurrent.futures module

The concurrent.futures module is designed for programs that can be structured with one controlling process and several worker processes, where the controlling process hands out jobs to worker processes and then collects and collates the results. The following simple code example of a CPU-bound task uses the concurrent.futures module:

```python
from concurrent import futures

def factorize(n):
    """Return the prime factors of *n*

    This is a **very** bad factoring algorithm, which makes it a good
    example of a CPU bound task.

    """
    n = int(n)

    if n == 1:
        return 1, []

    found = []

    for i in range(2, (n // 2) + 1):
        if n % i == 0:
            if all(i % j != 0 for j in found):
                found.append(i)

    if not found:
        return n, [n]

    return n, found

if __name__ == '__main__':
    with futures.ProcessPoolExecutor() as pool:
        for number, factors in pool.map(factorize, range(1, 10001)):
            print('{}: {}'.format(number, factors))
```

That's a fairly generic model, especially, for CPU-bound programs. So, `concurrent.futures` is as widely applicable as it is simple to use, and the preceding code example shows that it is simple.

The basic usage is to just import it, create a `ProcessPoolExecutor` object, and then call that object's `map` or `submit` methods to send work to the worker processes. When we're completely done with the `ProcessPoolExecutor` and we know we'll never need it again, we call its `shutdown` method or allow the `with` statement to do it for us. The `ProcessPoolExecutor` object will take care of all the twitchy little details of creating and communicating with the worker processes.

Before going ahead with the `map` and `submit` methods, let's find out more about `ProcessPoolExecutor` and what it does.

Calling ProcessPoolExecutor

When we call the `ProcessPoolExecutor` map or submit methods (which we'll discuss later in this section), we're asking it to call a function with the given parameters. But we want that function call to happen inside a worker process. This has some implications that might not be obvious:

- First of all, it means that the function and its parameters need to be **picklable**, which is another way of saying that Python needs to know how to turn them into a byte string that it could send to the worker process.

  For functions, that basically means any function is OK, unless it was defined within the body of another function.

  For the parameters, it means that most objects will work, but generators and a few other kinds of special object can't be passed.

 Being aware that both the function and the parameters passed to it can easily bring along information we didn't intend to send when they get pickled for communication to the worker processes is important.

If any of the objects we sent to the `ProcessPoolExecutor` object references other objects, those objects get pickled up and sent too. It's entirely possible to end up sending most of the state of our program. That's particularly worth noting when the function we're asking to run is a method of an object.

If the function is a method of an object, the whole object will get pickled and sent to the worker process, which means that the function call will be happening with a copy of the original object as its self-parameter, not the original object.

- Second, the return value of the function is pickled and returned to the controlling process. All of the warnings about passing parameters to the called function applied to the return value too.

 So, for example, if the function can't return a generator object and its return value contains references to a bunch of objects, copies of them will end up being sent to the controlling process.

- Third and finally, the `concurrent.futures` code that's running in the worker processes needs to be able to import the modules that our original code was loaded from.

 This means that we may need to use the `if __name__ == '__main__'` trick to keep the worker processes from getting stuck running complete copies of our program, when all they wanted to do was import the module and find the function we were asking to have run.

We already saw the `map` method of `ProcessPoolExecutor` in our example, but let's look a little closer.

Using the map method

The map method takes a function as its first parameter. We can also pass it one or more intervals, which will be used to figure out the parameters for each call to the function:

```
from concurrent import futures

def foo(x, y):
    return y - x

with futures.ProcessPoolExecutor() as pool:
    pool.map(foo, [1, 2, 3], [4, 5, 6])

<<< means >>>

foo(1, 4)
foo(2, 5)
foo(3, 6)
```

Refer to the preceding code example, if we ask `pool` to map the `foo` function to the list `[1, 2, 3]` and `[4, 5, 6]`, the result is that the `foo` function will be called with 1 and 4 as its parameters, called again with 2 and 5 as its parameters, and called a third time with 3 and 6 as its parameters.

 There's no guarantee in which order these three calls will happen, though. After all, they're likely to each run in different processes and the relationship between process scheduling and wall-clock time is partly dependent on unpredictable factors.

The map method hides that fact by waiting for all the calls to finish and produce the results, then returning an iterator over those results in the proper order.

Using the submit method

Sometimes, the map method is too simple. What if we want to handle the results as each worker produces them, instead of waiting for all the workers to get done? What if we decide not to run the function after all? What if we want to run different functions in worker processes at the same time? For that matter, what if we want to pass keyword arguments to the function? We could do all that and more using the submit method.

Each call to the submit method translates to a single call to the function that we pass as the first parameter of the submit method. The rest of the parameters and keyword arguments we pass to submit are passed into the function after being sent to the worker process.

Let's look at an example of the `submit` method in action:

```
    This is a **very** bad factoring algorithm, which makes it a good
    example of a CPU bound task.

    """
    n = int(n)

    if n < 2:
        raise ValueError('Invalid number for factorization', n)

    found = []

    for i in range(2, (n // 2) + 1):
        if n % i == 0:
            if all(i % j != 0 for j in found):
                found.append(i)

    if not found:
        return n, [n]

    return n, found
if __name__ == '__main__':
    with futures.ProcessPoolExecutor() as pool:
        fs = [pool.submit(factorize, x) for x in range(1, 10001)]
        for f in futures.as_completed(fs):
            try:
                number, factors = f.result()
            except ValueError:
                continue
            print('{}: {}'.format(number, factors))
```

So, for each time we call `submit`, one worker process calls one function with one set of parameters. The `submit` method does not wait for the worker process to finish running the function before returning. In fact, it doesn't even wait for the worker process to start running the function and so `submit` does not return the result of the called function. Instead, it returns a `future` object.

 A `future` object is in some sense an IOU for the result of the function. If we have a `future` object, we can use it to check whether the worker process has finished running the function to get the result returned by the function or even to set up a callback that will be called when the function finally does finish running. We can even use the `future` object to remove the function call from the queue of jobs that should be shared out to the worker.

The `done` and `result` methods of a `future` object are the ones we'll use most often.

The done and result methods

The `done` method returns `true` if the job is done and `false` if it's not. A job is done if it was cancelled, if it raised an exception, or if the job function has returned, as shown in the following code example:

```
from concurrent import futures

class FooError(Exception):
    pass

def foo(x, y):
    if x > y:
        raise FooError
    return y - x

with futures.ProcessPoolExecutor() as pool:
    future = pool.submit(foo, 4, 7)

    while not future.done():
        ... do other stuff ...

    try:
        data = future.result()
    except FooError:
        data = None
```

The `result` method returns the return value of the job function if it completed successfully. If the job function raised an exception instead of returning a value, the worker process will catch the exception and hand it back to the controlling process as the result of the job.

In the preceding code example, calling the `result` method will re-raise the exception, so it can be handled properly.

The timeout parameter

The timeout parameter is an important parameter in the `result` method. It is useful if we want to call the `result` method before the job is done.

If we call the `result` method before the job function is done, then the `result` method will wait for the job to complete before it returns. This could be very useful, but sometimes we don't want to wait indefinitely. If the job isn't done quickly, we want to go on and do something else for a while.

In such a case, we should pass the number of seconds we're willing to wait to the `timeout` parameter of the `result` method, as shown in the following code example:

```
from concurrent import futures

class FooError(Exception):
    pass

def foo(x, y):
    if x > y:
        raise FooError
    return y - x

with futures.ProcessPoolExecutor() as pool:
    future = pool.submit(foo, 4, 7)

    while not future.done():
        ... do other stuff ...

    while True:
        try:
            data = future.result(timeout = 0.5)
        except futures.TimeoutError:
            print('Working...')
            continue
        except FooError:
            data = None

        break
```

Along with the `timeout` parameter, we will add a `TimeoutError` exception. If the `timeout` parameter expires without a result being produced, a timeout error will be raised.

The wait and as_completed functions

There is a pair of functions in the `concurrent.futures` package that let's wait on several futures at once. They're called `wait` and `as_completed`. The following code example represents the `wait` function:

```
from concurrent import futures

class FooError(Exception):
    pass

def foo(x, y):
    if x > y:
        raise FooError
    return y - x

with futures.ProcessPoolExecutor() as pool:
    running = [pool.submit(foo, 5, 8),
               pool.submit(foo, 6, 9)]

    while running:
        done, running = futures.wait(running, timeout = 2.5)
        for future in done:
            data = future.result()
            ... do whatever we need with data ...
```

The `wait` function waits until all the `futures` are ready to deliver the results or until a timeout expires. Then, it returns a set of `futures` that are done and a set of `futures` that aren't. In contrast, the `as_completed` function returns an iterator that produces `futures` one by one as they become ready to produce the results.

In rare cases, the `done` and `result` methods of future and the `wait` and `as_completed` functions of the `concurrent.futures` package aren't sufficient to let a program process futures at the proper times.

For those occasions, it's possible to have the `future` call a function when the result becomes available. We can do that by passing a function into the `add done callback` method of `future`.

The add done callback function

The `future` object will remember that function and when the `job` function is done, the `callback` function will be called with the `future` object as its only parameter. The code in the `callback` function can then call the future's `result` method to get the return value or exception that the job produced.

 The `callback` function will always be called in the controlling process, but it might not be called in the same thread as the main part of the program.

When we use `add done callback`, we need to be careful of thread synchronization issues, which is a big reason to prefer the `wait` or `as_completed` functions when possible. The `future` objects also have a `cancel` method.

The cancel method

The `cancel` method tries to tell the system that we don't want the call to happen after all (refer to the following code example):

```python
from concurrent import futures

class FooError(Exception):
    pass

def foo(x, y):
    if x > y:
        raise FooError
    return y - x

with futures.ProcessPoolExecutor() as pool:
    running = [pool.submit(foo, 5, 8),
               pool.submit(foo, 6, 9)]

    if running[0].cancel():
        print('Successfully cancelled')
    else:
        print('Too late')
```

This code example is not guaranteed to work because if a worker process has already begun a job, that job is no longer cancellable.

- If the job connected to a `future` object can't be cancelled, the `cancel` method returns `false`
- If the cancellation succeeded, the `cancel` method returns `true`

The `concurrent.futures` module is perfectly suited to farming out computational tasks to multiple processes to take advantage of the CPU power of multicore and multiprocessor computers. The `map`, `submit`, `wait`, and `as_completed` functions are usually all you need for that kind of task.

Using the multiprocessing packages

In the previous section, we saw that the `concurrent.futures` package makes it very simple to farm out computational jobs to worker processes. If the program we need doesn't fit into the *send out jobs and collect the results* model, we're probably better off working at a somewhat lower level of abstraction.

So, let's now move on to look at another package that helps us handle multiprocess programs that don't fit that model, but the pieces are only partly independent of each other. From time to time, they need to pass information between themselves, not just back to the controlling process. We can't do that with `concurrent.futures` because it just doesn't fit into the model that `concurrent.futures` uses to describe parallel processing.

Alternatively, what if we need to be able to cancel a job after a worker process has started running it? Again, that doesn't fit the `concurrent.futures` model. The `concurrent.futures` model is powerful, but its power is based in simplicity and so it's not too hard to imagine scenarios it can't handle.

When we need to build our own model of how parallel processing should work, we can use the `multiprocessing` module as the foundation.

Process class in the multiprocessing module

The `multiprocessing` module contains a class called `Process` that represents the ability to run code in a separate process.

Probably the simplest way to use the `Process` class is to subclass it and override the `run` method, which is the entry point for code in the other process, as shown in this code example:

```
from multiprocessing import Process

class Squares(Process):
    def run(self):
        for i in range(10):
            print(i ** 2)

squares = Squares()

squares.start()
```

In the preceding example, we created a specific kind of process that calculates some square numbers. Then, we created an instance and started running it. When we called `start`, the `multiprocessing` module did the necessary work to make sure that the `run` method was executed in a new process.

By the way, all of the warnings we discussed in the `concurrent.futures` module section (*Using the concurrent.futures package*) about pickling and importing modules applies to the `multiprocessing` module as well. When it comes to moving data between processes and importing code, they work in the same way.

So far, we haven't seen anything that we couldn't do better with `concurrent.futures`, but it changes when we start using **queues**, **pipes**, and **managers**. Let's have a look at them in detail.

Queues

Queues are communication channels that are appropriate for one to many, many to one, and many to many communications between cooperating processes. Depending on how they're used, that makes them ideal for posting tasks to a worker process when we don't care which worker ends up doing the task and for collecting the results of multiple worker processes.

Any process can put a picklable object into a queue and any process can remove the next available object from the queue.

Queues are **First In First Out** (**FIFO**) data structures, which means that objects are removed from the queue in the same order that they're added. The `JoinableQueue` class adds a method, which allows a process to wait until the queue has been emptied by other processes. OK, let's take a closer look at `queue` objects:

```
from queue import Empty
from multiprocessing import Queue
from multiprocessing import JoinableQueue

q = Queue()

q.put('hello')

result = q.get()

try:
    data = q.get_nowait()
except Empty:
    data = None

try:
    more = q.get(timeout = 2.5)
except Empty:
    more = None
```

Refer to the preceding code example; there are three methods that are primarily useful: `put`, `get`, and `get_nowait`.

- When we call `put`, an object is placed at the back of the queue.
- When we call `get`, an object is removed from the queue and returned, unless the queue is empty. If the queue is empty, the process that called `get` waits until it is able to remove and return an object, which will happen after some other process puts an object into the queue.
- When we call `get_nowait` on the other hand, it either removes and returns the object at the front of the queue or it raises a `q.empty` exception.
- Finally, we could pass a `timeout` parameter to the `get` method, in which case it will either remove and return an object within that many seconds or raise `q.empty`.

We could pass queue objects around between processes by making them part of the process's initial data, or by sending them through pre-existing queues or pipes, or even by storing them in a manager. Queues are designed to be shared between processes. Moving on, let's look at pipes.

Pipes

Pipes are one-to-one communication channels. When we call a pipe, we get back a pair of objects that each serve as one end of the communication stream. If we give one end each to a pair of processes, they could send messages and data back and forth through the pipe.

Each end of the pipe has the same methods. The interesting methods are `send`, `recv`, and `poll`. Consider the following code example:

```
from multiprocessing import Pipe

near, far = Pipe()

# ... Pass far on to a different process ...

near.send(('hello', 5))

if near.poll(timeout = 2.5):
    data = near.recv()
```

In the preceding code example, we see these:

- The `send` method accepts an object as its parameter and sends it to the other endpoint.
- The `recv` method waits for something to be sent from the other endpoint, and then returns it.
- The `poll` method returns `true` if there's an object way to be received and `false` if there is not.

The `poll` method can accept a `timeout` parameter. If we give it a number for the timeout and there's not currently anything waiting to be received, the `poll` function will wait for up to that many seconds for data to arrive and then return `true`. If no data arrives before the timeout expires, the `poll` method will return `false`.

If we pass `None` as the `poll` method's `timeout` parameter, it will wait until data arrives before returning, no matter how long it takes. Like queue objects, pipe endpoints can be sent to other processes as they're launched or through other queues, pipes, and so on after the process is running.

Using queues and pipes as the only connection between the processes is usually considered best because this maximizes the ability of the processes to work in parallel.

If it's possible to organize a parallel program that way, it should be. If we find that we need to share some variables between several processes though, we can do it using a `Manager` object. Let's look at manager now.

Manager

A manager represents a special process with only one job-keeping track of the variables that other processes need.

 Accessing variables stored in a manager is much slower than accessing a process's local variables and it could lead to situations where processes trying to access variables at the same time slow each other down. On the other hand, if we actually need shared variables, at least the manager handles them correctly and as efficiently as possible.

Now, managers can handle many types of data, but we're going to focus on their ability to store **dictionaries**, **lists**, and **namespaces**.

Normally, when we send an object to another process, the other process actually gets a copy of that object; this means if the other process changes the object it receives, we don't see those changes in the original process.

A manager lets us create objects that behave more like queues in that, if we send the object to another process and that process changes the object, we do see the changes in the original process or any other process that has access to the object. Consider this code example:

```
from multiprocessing import Manager

manager = Manager()

dictionary = manager.dict()
sequence = manager.list()
obj = manager.Namespace()

dictionary['hello'] = 'world'
sequence.append(57)
obj.attribute = 'This is shared data'

lock = manager.Lock()
event = manager.Event()
cond = manager.Condition()
sem = manager.BoundedSemaphore(3)
```

The `manager.dict()` and `manager.list()` methods in the preceding code example create special dictionaries or lists that could be shared between processes. The `Namespace` method, which does indeed start with a capital `N`, creates a more generic shared object on which we can set attributes to share them between processes.

When we have shared data that is being accessed by multiple streams of execution, which is exactly what manager provides, we have to be careful to keep the data access synchronized. To help with that, managers can also create some standard synchronization primitives, such as **locks**, **events**, **conditions**, and **semaphores**.

The lock object

Lock objects are the simplest of the synchronization tools. They have a pair of methods called `acquire` and `release`, as shown in the following code example:

```
from multiprocessing import Manager

manager = Manager()

lock = manager.Lock()

lock.acquire()

# ... manipulate data ...

lock.release()
```

After a process calls `acquire`, any other process that calls `acquire` is forced to wait until the first process calls `release`. Then, the `acquire` call in one of the waiting processes returns, allowing that process to proceed. In other words, code between an `acquire` call and `release` call can count on being the only code accessing whatever data the `lock` object is protecting.

Notice that the `lock` object doesn't know what data it's protecting. It's up to us as programmers to define and respect that association in our own minds.

The event object

Event objects allow a process to proceed immediately if a flag is `true` or wait until the flag becomes `true`.

The flag is set to `false` by calling the `event.clear` method or `true` by calling its `event.set` method, as shown in this code example:

```
from multiprocessing import Manager

manager = Manager()

event = manager.Event()

event.clear()
event.wait()

# In a different process

event.set()
```

When we call the `event.wait` method, it will return immediately if the flag is `true` else it will pause execution until another process calls `set` and then return.

Event objects are useful for making a process pause until some specific thing happens.

The condition object

The condition objects combine some of the features of `lock` and `event` objects. Like a `lock`, they have `acquire` and `release` methods that can be used to protect data from simultaneous access.

However, a `condition` object also has a `wait` method and a `notify` method, which can be used to wait until some other process does something and to wake up a waiting process as shown in the following code example:

```
from multiprocessing import Manager

manager = Manager()

cond = manager.Condition()

cond.acquire()
cond.wait()

# ... manipulate data ...

cond.release()

# in another process

cond.acquire()

# ... manipulate data ...

cond.notify()
cond.release()
```

Condition objects are useful for creating data structures that synchronize access to their contents and wait when they don't have any data to return. The `get` and `put` methods of the `queue` class could be implemented using a `condition` object.

The semaphore object

The `semaphore` objects look a lot like `lock` objects. The difference is that, where the `lock` objects always ensured that exactly one process has acquired the lock at a given time, `semaphore` objects ensure that no more than a fixed number of processes can acquire it at the same time.

This can be seen using the following code example:

```
from multiprocessing import Manager

manager = Manager()

sem = manager.BoundedSemaphore(3)

sem.acquire()

# ... access limited resource ...

sem.release()
```

This is useful for doing things such as limiting the number of worker processes that can access the hard disk at the same time.

Summary

In this chapter, you learned how to use `concurrent.futures` to make a particularly common multiprocess case extremely simply. We also saw how to use the `multiprocessing` package to define what worker processes do and how they interact.

So, now we know quite a lot about how to help CPU-bound programs take advantage of multicore and multiprocessor hardware to run faster. Most programs aren't CPU-bound though, they're I/O-bound, which means they spend most of their time waiting for input from various sources. Parallel processing doesn't help in that situation, but asynchronous I/O does, and that's the topic for our next chapter.

7
Coroutines and Asynchronous I/O

In the previous chapter, we looked at how to use multiple processes to increase the rate of data processing in our programs. This is great for CPU-bound programs because it allows them to use more than one CPU.

In this chapter, we'll look at the inverse of this case; we'll use a single CPU to handle multiple data processing tasks at once within a single process, which is great for I/O-bound programs. We'll see some of the nuts and bolts of working with asyncio. We'll also discuss asyncio's `future` class and how it's used. Then we'll move on to synchronization and communication between asynchronous coroutine tasks. Lastly, we'll see how to use asyncio and coroutines to write a client-server program to communicate over a network.

We will cover the following topics:

- The difference between asynchronous processing and parallel processing
- Using the asyncio event loop and coroutine scheduler
- Waiting for data to become available
- Synchronizing multiple tasks
- Communicating across a network

The difference between asynchronous processing and parallel processing

When we worked with the `concurrent.futures` module in Chapter 6, *Parallel Processing*, we saw a way to make two or more streams of code run at the same time. For reference, have a look at the code example we used in the previous chapter:

```python
from concurrent import futures

def factorize(n):
    """Return the prime factors of *n*

    This is a **very** bad factoring algorithm, which makes it a good
    example of a CPU bound task.

    """
    n = int(n)

    if n < 2:
        raise ValueError('Invalid number for factorization', n)

    found = []

    for i in range(2, (n // 2) + 1):
        if n % i == 0:
            if all(i % j != 0 for j in found):
                found.append(i)

    if not found:
        return n, [n]

    return n, found

if __name__ == '__main__':
    with futures.ProcessPoolExecutor() as pool:
        fs = [pool.submit(factorize, x) for x in range(1, 10001)]
        for f in futures.as_completed(fs):
```

This code helps you create an executor object. Now if you ever wish to run some code in parallel, you could just tell the executor to do it. The executor would give us a future object that we could use later to get the result of the code, and it would then run the code in a separate process. Our original code will keep on running in the original process.

We talked about how this could improve the performance of CPU-bound programs—it divides the code into multiple computer cores. Therefore, it's a technique that would be convenient in a lot of other circumstances.

It's handy to be able to tell the computer to "go do this and let me know when you're done".

One place where this ability seems particularly useful is in network server programs, where having a separate stream of execution for each connected client makes the logic and structure of the code much easier to grasp; it's easier to write bug-free servers when they're structured this way.

Multithreading is not good for servers

There are ways to write a server that would use only a single stream of execution, but if we have a way of writing servers that would probably introduce fewer bugs, why not? The problem is resource overhead.

Every process running on a computer uses up memory and CPU time, of course; however, in addition to the memory and CPU time, the process needs to run its code as well. The operating system also needs to expend some resources to manage the process. As it happens, the time spent on switching between processes is significant.

Memory overhead is enough; it becomes a limiting factor for how many clients a multiprocess server can handle simultaneously; other internal operating system resources may be even more limiting.

For CPU-bound programs, there's a sweet spot that produces optimal results, where the program has one process per CPU core. For an I/O-bound program, which most servers are, any process beyond the first is nothing but overhead. As mentioned, there are ways to write single-process servers that can handle multiple clients at once with much lower overhead per connected client.

These techniques allow a server to handle many more clients at once than what the multiprocess server program could manage. Even when not operating at full capacity, a single-process server leaves the majority of a computer's resources available for other uses.

So, on one hand, we have a way of writing servers that is logically structured and less prone to bugs but wastes resources. On the other hand, we have a way of writing servers that is resource efficient but easy to get wrong.

Can we somehow get the best of both the worlds? The answer is, yes!

Fortunately, Python's standard `asyncio` module combines low-level techniques that allow a single process to service multiple clients with a cooperative coroutine scheduler. Refer to the following code example:

```python
import asyncio

async def example():
    x = await do_stuff()
    return 'Hello world', x

async def very_long():
    while True:
        await asyncio.sleep(0)
```

The end result is a programming interface that looks and acts a lot like `concurrent.futures` but with much lower overhead per stream of code execution. That's great, but what's a cooperative coroutine scheduler? For that matter, what's a coroutine?

Cooperative coroutine scheduler versus coroutine

Before we get into detail, let's define these two terms:

- A coroutine is a computer science concept, a function that can be paused and resumed at certain intervals within it. Each time it is paused, it sends data out, and each time it is resumed, it receives data.

  Python programs can define coroutines using the async and await keywords, and asyncio makes extensive use of them.

- A cooperative coroutine scheduler is a piece of code that picks up the execution each time a coroutine pauses and decides which coroutine to run next. It's called a scheduler because it keeps track of multiple streams of execution and decides which one gets to run at any given time.

  It's called cooperative because the scheduler can't run from one coroutine to another while the first one is still running. It has to wait until the running coroutine pauses itself, then it can select another coroutine to run.

Python coroutines

In Python coroutines, the pause and resume points are `await` expressions; this is how we call other coroutines. Every time we want to perform a function, we call a coroutine from inside another coroutine. We wait for the coroutine we want to call.

The semantics of the code work as if they call a function from inside another function. The other coroutine runs until it returns and we get back the return value. That's how the code behaves, but what it actually does is quite a bit more interesting.

The coroutine scheduler

With the coroutine scheduler, the code behaves in the following manner:

- The first thing that happens is that the coroutine we're running is paused. The coroutine we want to call is handed on to the scheduler, which places it in its list of coroutines that it needs to run.
- Then, the scheduler checks whether a coroutine is waiting and why: for example, new data coming from across the network, or a coroutine being returned; if it's the latter, it adds the waiting coroutines to the list as well.
- After this, the scheduler picks one of the coroutines that needs to be run and resumes it. This means that if a coroutine has a long-running loop that doesn't contain any `await` expressions, it will block any other coroutine from running. It will also keep the program from checking for new incoming data and prevent other assorted input and output operations from being serviced.

If we have such a loop and there's just no reason to call any other coroutine inside it, we can place the `await asyncio.sleep(0)` statement inside the loop body, which simply gives the scheduler a chance to do its thing.

This little bit of extra complexity that comes from the requirement of having `await` expressions is the price of cooperative scheduling, but since the payoff is efficient and logical code for I/O-bound programs, it's often worth it.

Using the asyncio event loop and coroutine scheduler

So far, you have learned about Python's coroutines and a bit about how a cooperative coroutine scheduler works. Now, let's try our hand at writing some asynchronous code using Python coroutines and asyncio. We start this by creating a coroutine.

Creating a coroutine

It's easy to create a coroutine—all we have to do is use the `async` keyword on a function and use `await` anytime we want to call other coroutines, as shown in following code example:

```
import asyncio

async def example():
    await asyncio.sleep(5)
    return 5
```

Once we have a coroutine though, we can't just call it to get the ball rolling. If we try to call it, it immediately returns a `coroutine` object, as shown in the following code example—that's not much use:

```
>>> import coroutine
>>> coroutine.example()
<coroutine object example at 0x7f3c6bebd570>
>>>
```

Instead, we need to add the coroutine to the asyncio's scheduler as a new task. Next, the scheduler runs arranging for coroutines to execute and handling input and output events.

The asyncio scheduler - event_loop

The `asyncio` package automatically creates a default scheduler, also called `event_loop`.

While it's possible to create new `event_loop` objects or replace the default one, for our purposes, the default `event_loop` scheduler will work just fine. We could get a reference to it by calling asyncio's `get_event_loop` function to tell the scheduler that we want it to start a new task, as shown here:

```
>>> import asyncio
>>> scheduler = asyncio.get_event_loop()
>>> f = asyncio.ensure_future(coroutine.example())
>>> f
__main__:1: RuntimeWarning: coroutine 'example' was never awaited
<Task pending coro=<example() running at /home/devesh/coroutine.py:3>>
>>>
```

When we run the preceding coroutine, we call asyncio's `ensure_future` function. By default, this will create the task in the default scheduler.

ensure_future

We can also override default scheduler by passing an explicit `event_loop` scheduler to the loop keyword-only parameter of the `ensure_future` function.

```
f = asyncio.ensure_future(coroutine.example(),  loop = scheduler)
```

Notice that we didn't just pass the `coroutine` function to `ensure_future`; we actually invoked it right there inside `ensure_future` arguments. We did this because the `ensure_future` function doesn't actually want to refer to the `coroutine` function. The `ensure_future` function is only interested in the `coroutine` object that we saw the `coroutine` function return earlier. The name `ensure_future` might seem somewhat odd. If it's used for launching tasks, why is it called that?

The fact of the matter is that launching tasks is basically just a side effect of what the function conceptually does, which is **wrapping**. Wrap the function's parameter in a future object if necessary. It just so happens that having a future object for the return value of our coroutine would be useless if the coroutine is never scheduled to run; `ensure_future` makes sure that it does.

The `ensure_future` function adds a new task to the scheduler, whether it's called from normal code or within a coroutine. This means that any time we want the code to run in its own stream of execution, we can use `ensure_future` to get it going.

Even in the preceding code example, where we added a coroutine to the scheduler as a new task, nothing happened. That's because the scheduler itself is still not running. However, this is an easily solvable problem. We just need to call either the `run_forever` or `run_until_complete` method of the loop. Finally, our coroutine would actually execute, as shown here:

```
scheduler.run_until_complete(f)
5
```

The run_forever/run_until_complete methods

As the names implies, `run_forever` causes `event_loop` to run forever or at least until it's explicitly stopped by calling its `stop` method. On the other hand, the `run_until_complete` method causes the loop to keep going until a particular future object is ready to provide a value (refer to the following code example):

```python
import asyncio
import logging

async def coro1():
    while True:
        for i in range(100000):
            await asyncio.sleep(0.1)
        print('coro1')

async def coro2():
    for i in range(25):
        await asyncio.sleep(0.5)
        print(i)

    loop = asyncio.get_event_loop()
    loop.stop()


logging.getLogger('asyncio').setLevel('CRITICAL')

asyncio.ensure_future(coro1())
asyncio.ensure_future(coro2())

loop = asyncio.get_event_loop()
loop.run_forever()
loop.close()
```

The return value of `ensure_future` is a future object, so you can easily run the scheduler until a particular task is done. The preceding code example runs two coroutines simultaneously as two separate tasks in the same scheduler. The `coro1()` coroutine contains an infinite loop, so it will never finish; however, the `coro2()` coroutine not only finishes, it also causes the `event_loop` stop method's (`loop.stop ()`) to force `run_forever` to terminate eventually. This is shown in the following code example:

```python
import asyncio
import logging

async def coro1():
    while True:
        for i in range(100000):
            await asyncio.sleep(0.1)
        print('coro1')

async def coro2():
    for i in range(25):
        await asyncio.sleep(0.5)
        print(i)

logging.getLogger('asyncio').setLevel('CRITICAL')

asyncio.ensure_future(coro1())
f = asyncio.ensure_future(coro2())

loop = asyncio.get_event_loop()
loop.run_until_complete(f)
loop.close()
```

The preceding example behaves in exactly the same way, except it uses `run_until_complete` to automatically stop the scheduler once `coro2` is finished instead of explicitly calling `stop`.

The code looks a little cleaner this way. So, as a rule of thumb, it's probably better to only use stop when some sort of error makes it necessary to dump out of `event_loop`. In both the examples we just saw, there's a line of code to set the logging level to critical. This is because `event_loop` issues an error message if it is stopped while there are tasks, such as `coro1`, still running. In this case, we know it's still running and we don't care, so we suppress the message.

It's usually better to arrange for all our running tasks to exit cleanly, instead of just killing them. This is why the error message is printed. But, in our case, there's no problem, so we just keep the message from printing.

Regardless of how we choose to run and stop `event_loop`, once we're completely finished with it, we should call its `close` method. It closes any open files, network sockets, and other I/O channels that `event_loop` is managing and generally cleans up after itself.

Closing event_loop

A good way to close `event_loop` is to use the `contextlib.closing` context manager, which guarantees that the `close` method will be called once the `with` block ends. The following code example shows `event_loop` closing:

```python
import asyncio
import logging
import contextlib

async def coro1():
    while True:
        for i in range(100000):
            await asyncio.sleep(0.1)
        print('coro1')

async def coro2():
    for i in range(25):
        await asyncio.sleep(0.5)
        print(i)

logging.getLogger('asyncio').setLevel('CRITICAL')

asyncio.ensure_future(coro1())
f = asyncio.ensure_future(coro2())

with contextlib.closing(asyncio.get_event_loop()) as loop:
    loop.run_until_complete(f)
```

Even in error situations, the `close` method should be called when we're completely done with an `event_loop`, but this doesn't necessarily mean that it should be called right after the `run_forever` or `run_until_complete` call is finished. The `event_loop` is still in a valid state at that point, and it's perfectly OK to, for example, add some new tasks or start the loop again.

As you may have probably noticed, an `asyncio event_loop` object basically fulfills the same role as a `concurrent.futures executor` object. From a programming interface point of view, that's not the only similarity.

Awaiting data availability

asyncio's future objects look and behave pretty much like `concurrent.futures` future objects, but they're not interchangeable. They have subtle differences in behavior and, of course, major differences in how they interact with the underlying systems, which are completely different. Still, each future is a way of referencing the value that may or may not have been computed yet and, if necessary, a way of waiting for that value to become available.

asyncio's future objects

The most commonly used feature of a future object is to wait for its value to be determined and then retrieve it. For asyncio's future objects, this is done by simply waiting for the future, as shown in the following code example:

```
import asyncio

async def get_future_values(future1, future2):
    value1 = await future1
    value2 = future2.result() if future2.done() else None
    return value1, value2
```

This will tell the scheduler to pause the coroutine until the value of the future becomes available, after which the future's value is set in the coroutine as the result of the `await` expression.

If the future represents a raised exception, instead of a value, that exception is raised again from the `await` expression, as shown in the preceding code example. If we don't want to wait, we could call the `done` method to check whether a future is ready; if it is, we could call the `result` method to retrieve the value.

So, the syntax and semantics are a little different, but the basic idea of a future is the same in asyncio and `concurrent.futures`. When we work with asyncio, we use future objects in all the same places we would in `concurrent.futures`.

There's one scenario where even using future objects doesn't make it simple to wait for data; this is when we should process a stream of data values as they arrive, as shown here:

```python
import asyncio

class SlowSequence:
    class Iterator:
        def __init__(self, slowseq):
            self.values = list(slowseq.values)

        async def __anext__(self):
            await asyncio.sleep(2)
            try:
                return self.values.pop(0)
            except IndexError:
                raise StopAsyncIteration

    def __init__(self, *values):
        self.values = values

    async def __aiter__(self):
        return SlowSequence.Iterator(self)

async def main():
    seq = SlowSequence(1, 2, 3, 4, 5)

    async for value in seq:
        print(value)

loop = asyncio.get_event_loop()
loop.run_until_complete(asyncio.ensure_future(main()))
loop.close()
```

Sure, we could loop over an iterator of future objects and wait for each one of them to become ready to provide their values, but that's clumsy and suffers from problems in regard to knowing when to stop the iteration.

Instead, Python provides us with an asynchronous iteration protocol, which allows us to write or fetch the next value function as a coroutine. This means that the iterator can wait for each value to arrive and simply return it. Now our loop will work properly and we will avoid all the confusion about when to stop.

Asynchronous iterations

Why do we need a special asynchronous iteration for a looping statement and a separate asynchronous iteration protocol?

It's because an asynchronous iteration only makes sense inside of a coroutine. Having a separate looping statement and protocol keeps us from stumbling into ambiguous situations, where the computer isn't sure what we want it to do.

Synchronizing multiple tasks

In this section, we'll take a look at more ways to share data between tasks and synchronize their operations.

Synchronization primitives

The `asyncio` package provides `lock`, `semaphore`, `event`, and `condition` classes that are pretty similar to the ones we looked at in the context of `concurrent.futures`. They provide the same method names and fulfill the same roles. The important difference is that for asyncio's versions, some of the methods are coroutines and some are not, as shown here:

```
>>> asyncio.iscoroutinefunction(asyncio.Lock.acquire)
True
>>> asyncio.iscoroutinefunction(asyncio.Lock.release)
False
>>> asyncio.iscoroutinefunction(asyncio.Condition.wait)
True
>>> asyncio.iscoroutinefunction(asyncio.Condition.wait_for)
True
>>> asyncio.iscoroutinefunction(asyncio.Semaphore.acquire)
True
>>> asyncio.iscoroutinefunction(asyncio.Semaphore.release)
False
>>>
```

Specifically, in each case, the `acquire` and `wait` methods, if they exist, are coroutines that must be called by `await`.

This is because they need to be able to pause until some specific thing happens, and only a coroutine can pause and hand over control to the scheduler. Having mentioned lock and the rest, I want to point out that while they are sometimes necessary, they are less often needed under asyncio than they would be in concurrent.futures or other systems that provide multiple streams of execution.

This is because asyncio's scheduling is cooperative. It's only possible to switch between execution streams and `await` expressions, which means that if there are no await expressions within a critical section of code, it can't be interrupted.

 No other task can modify the same data at the same time because no other task has an opportunity to run any code during that time. Plus, Lock and the rest are only needed when a critical section of the code does, in fact, use `await` at least once.

We've seen the `as_completed` and `wait` functions before when we discussed concurrent.futures in the previous chapter. asyncio's versions are coroutines because they too need to suspend until it's time to continue executing, but there's not much of a difference in how we use them.

The wait coroutine

The wait coroutine still waits for a group of futures to end with an optional timeout and returns a list of futures that are ready and a list of futures that are not ready when the time expires. The `as_completed` function still takes a list of futures and produces futures of the results in the order that the results become available. Then, we extract the actual values from the futures with wait and we are good to go.

As shown in the following code example, there's no telling in which order the results will become available; however, each time a value does become available, it gets printed:

```python
import asyncio
import random

async def delayed_value(value):
    await asyncio.sleep(random.randrange(5))
    return value

async def main():
    futures = [
        asyncio.ensure_future(delayed_value(1)),
        asyncio.ensure_future(delayed_value(2)),
        asyncio.ensure_future(delayed_value(3)),
        asyncio.ensure_future(delayed_value(4)),
        asyncio.ensure_future(delayed_value(5)),
    ]

    for future in asyncio.as_completed(futures):
        value = await future
        print(value)

loop = asyncio.get_event_loop()
loop.run_until_complete(asyncio.ensure_future(main()))
loop.close()
```

asyncio provides some other interesting coroutines for collecting data from futures, particularly: wait_for and gather.

The wait_for coroutine

The `wait_for` coroutine lets us wait for another coroutine to finish but with a timeout. The first two coroutines in the following code example do the same thing except that if `foo` doesn't finish within 5 seconds, the second version will raise an asyncio timeout error:

```python
import asyncio

async def call_coro(coro):
    x = await coro()

async def call_coro_with_five_second_timeout(coro):
    x = await asyncio.wait_for(coro(), 5)

async def call_coro_with_timeout_and_handle_exception(coro):
    try:
        x = await asyncio.wait_for(coro(), 5)
    except asyncio.TimeoutError:
        print('Too slow')
```

In the third code block, we're still doing the same thing, except if `foo` times out, we print a message. Then, there's the `gather` coroutine.

The gather coroutine

What the `gather` coroutine does is it takes a bunch of futures and converts them into a single future that will be completed when all the subfutures are completed along with the result in the list of the subfutures' results, as shown in the following code example:

```python
import asyncio
import random

async def delayed_print(value):
    await asyncio.sleep(random.randrange(5))
    print(value)

main = asyncio.gather(
    asyncio.ensure_future(delayed_print(1)),
    asyncio.ensure_future(delayed_print(2)),
    asyncio.ensure_future(delayed_print(3)),
    asyncio.ensure_future(delayed_print(4)),
    asyncio.ensure_future(delayed_print(5)),
)

loop = asyncio.get_event_loop()
loop.run_until_complete(main)
loop.close()
```

There are a bunch of uses for something like that, but one very nice thing we can do with it is use it to construct the future that we pass into run_until_complete.

In effect, we're telling asyncio that it should run until all these futures are complete. Futures are great for communicating a one-off value between tasks, and events objects are good for sending simple signals. However, sometimes, we want a fully featured communication channel. Fortunately, asyncio provides us with the Queue class and a few variants based on it.

The asyncio Queue class

The asyncio's Queue has both put and get methods as coroutines. So, we need to call them with await and we have to already be in a coroutine to call them, unless we were to actually use the ensure_future function to launch them as separate tasks as shown in the following code example of the Queue class:

```
import asyncio

async def using_queues():
    q = asyncio.Queue()

    q.put_nowait('Hello')

    await q.get()

    await q.put('world')

    q.get_nowait()


    pq = asyncio.PriorityQueue()

    stack = asyncio.LifoQueue()
```

However, the Queue class also has methods called put_nowait and get_nowait, which are not coroutines, and can be called from anywhere. This makes the Queue class quite useful for communicating new data to a system of coroutines as well as sending data between coroutine tasks.

Queue types

asyncio provides a couple of variant Queue types that return their stored values in different orders.

Instances of PriorityQueue give back the smallest object they contain according to a less than comparison when we call get or get_nowait. So, if our priority queue contains 34, 2, 5, and 97, calling its get coroutine would return 2. The next time, it would return 5, then 34, and then 97.

A LifoQueue method, on the other hand, always gives back the most recently added object. It is, in other words, a stack data structure. asyncio also provides a joinable Queue class, which adds an extra join coroutine and a method called task_done. With a little bit of extra work, using a joinable queue allows coroutines to pause and wait until the queue is emptied.

Communicating across the network

So, we've covered how asyncio works and a bunch of tools that could be used to manage the execution of multiple streams of code. That's all great, but what about doing some actual I/O with it?

The primary motivation for people to use asynchronous I/O is because it helps when writing network clients and servers, although that's certainly not the only possible use. So, asyncio not only makes network communications efficient, it also makes them easy.

Creating a simple client in asyncio

Here, we have the code for a simple client-server pair of programs (refer to the following code example):

```
import asyncio
import itertools
import contextlib

async def client(host, port):
    reader, writer = await asyncio.open_connection(host, port)

    for i in itertools.count():
        writer.write(b'ping\n')
        response = await reader.readline()
        if response == b'pong\n':
            print(i)
        else:
            return

main = asyncio.ensure_future(client('127.0.0.1', 8899))
loop = asyncio.get_event_loop()

with contextlib.closing(loop):
    loop.run_until_complete(main)
```

```
import asyncio
import contextlib

async def serve(reader, writer):
    while True:
        try:
            request = await reader.readline()
        except ConnectionResetError:
            return
        if request == b'':
            return
        elif request == b'ping\n':
            writer.write(b'pong\n')
        else:
            writer.write(b'done\n')

async def launch(host, port):
    server = await asyncio.start_server(serve, host, port)
    await server.wait_closed()

main = asyncio.ensure_future(launch('127.0.0.1', 8899))
loop = asyncio.get_event_loop()

with contextlib.closing(loop):
    loop.run_until_complete(main)
```

They not only read and write the same few bytes over and over, but they also serve to demonstrate everything needed to communicate across the network.

There will be little information about the client that is mysterious.

Run the following command:

```
python3 client.py
```

It runs only a single task that uses asyncio's high-level API to open a connection and then send and receive data through it. The data is just a string of numbers as shown:

Creating a simple server in asyncio

The server can handle simultaneous connections from many clients at once because the `start_server` coroutine we called launches a new task to run the `start_serve` coroutine each time a client connects to the server.

Each task has the job of handling a connection to a single client, so the server coroutine is almost as simple as the client coroutine.

There's a little bit of extra code to handle a connection reset error, which is the exception that gets raised if the client suddenly disconnects while the server's trying to read data from it, and a little more to handle the class where the request is an empty string, which the readline coroutine can only produce if the client has closed the connection in a less precipitous manner.

Handling client disconnections

In both previous cases, we want the server to stop worrying about a particular client, which we can do simply by returning from the client handling coroutine. The task running the coroutine finishes and that's that.

In the launched coroutine on the server, we called another coroutine called `wait_closed`. That pretty much does what it says-it waits for the server to be closed. Without this call, our launched coroutine will immediately terminate and, since we used `run_until_complete`, the whole program will terminate immediately afterward.

This would happen because `start_server` launches a background task and then returns rather than manage the server directly, and that's about it.

There's a lower-level communication API that asyncio provides, but for the vast majority of cases, this lower-level API is unnecessary. asyncio makes network communications simple.

Summary

In the earlier sections of this chapter, we learned about coroutines, data exchange between coroutine tasks, and asynchronization. We had a look at using a future to wait for a single value or an asynchronous iterator, which may well use futures internally to wait for a sequence of values. We also looked at tools that we can use to transmit data to and from asynchronous coroutine tasks and force synchronization on them when necessary.

Now we've seen how to get a payoff from coroutines and asynchronization using these tools to write a network client or server. In the next chapter, we'll look at various parts of Python that can be redefined within our program source code and how to use them.

8

Metaprogramming

In the previous chapter, we discussed asynchronous I/O and coroutines. In this chapter, we turn our attention to metaprogramming and programmable syntax. We'll discuss various ways that Python allows us to control or alter the meaning of syntactic elements and use these features beneficially.

We'll look at another programmable syntax feature of Python that meshes nicely with function decorators. We'll also discuss class decorators and how they're similar to, and different from, function decorators. Then we'll see a different way of programmatically modifying classes using metaclasses. We'll move on to a less esoteric topic and discuss context managers. Finally, we'll look at one more way of programming the semantics of basic Python operations when we look at descriptors.

Metaprogramming is a blanket term for techniques where programs use program code or data structures constructed directly from program code as data to be manipulated. Python has a number of different features that can be thought of as metaprogramming.

In this chapter, we will cover the following topics:

- Using function decorators
- Function annotations
- Class decorators
- Metaclasses
- Context managers
- Descriptors

Using function decorators

In this section, we're going to look at one of the most ubiquitous **function decorators**. We'll see how to construct a decorator, how to use it, and how it works.

The basic definition of a decorator is simple. It's just a function that takes another function as its input, does something with it, and then returns the result of its operations, as shown here:

```
>>> def null_decorator(func):
...     return func
...
```

The return value replaces the original input function, so the changes a decorator can make are potentially quite drastic. A decorator that doesn't change anything at all is a function that accepts one parameter and immediately returns it.

Using the @ syntax in a function decorator

Python has a special syntax for applying a decorator to a function, using the @ syntax. With this syntax, we just write an @ symbol, followed by an expression that evaluates to a decorator function. We put that on the line right before the definition of the function we want to decorate, as shown in the following code example:

```
>>> @null_decorator
... def example():
...     print('hi')
...
```

This syntax means that as soon as we're done defining the function, we call the decorator function on it and then assign the return value of the decorator to the variable that would have contained the function, as shown here:

```
>>> # the above means
...
>>> def example():
...     print('hi')
...
>>> example = null_decorator(example)
>>>
>>> class Foo:
...     @staticmethod
...     def bar(x):
...         print(x)
...
>>> Foo.bar('stuff')
stuff
>>>
```

Global decorator - @staticmethod

Python includes a few decorators in the global namespace and an expanding list of them in the standard library. The most commonly used global decorator is @staticmethod. It makes the class member function callable through the class, rather than an instance, just like @staticmethod decorators in other languages. The following screenshot illustrates the code example for @staticmethod:

```
>>> def a(func):
...     print('a')
...     return func
...
>>> def b(func):
...     print('b')
...     return func
...
>>> @a
... @b
... def foo():
...     pass
...
b
a
>>> 
```

It's also possible to use multiple @ lines before `def`; with this, multiple decorators will be invoked. The decorator that's closest to `def` will be called first, and then its return value will be passed to the next closest decorator, and so on. Eventually, the return value of the topmost decorator will be assigned to the function's name in the containing scope, as shown in the following code example:

```
>>> def event_handler(func):
...     func.is_event_handler = True
...     return func
...
>>> @event_handler
... def foo(event):
...     pass
...
>>> if getattr(foo, 'is_event_handler', False):
...     print("It's an event handler")
...
It's an event handler
>>>
```

Attributes

One of the most common uses of decorators—in fact, the reason they're called decorators—is to add attributes to function objects. These attributes can be used by code in other parts of the program to distinguish decorated functions from each other and from under undecorated functions.

Adding attributes is easy. Inside the decorator, assign an attribute to the function, just like we would for any other object, and then return it. Then, elsewhere in the code, check for the attribute and respond accordingly.

That's all well and good and often quite useful, but we could do a lot more with decorators. For example, we can enclose the function in a wrapper that performs some computation before or after calling the function.

Enclosing the function in a wrapper

To enclose a function in a wrapper, first we want the function to find the wrapper inside a decorator (refer to the following code example). If you haven't seen this before, it is exactly how it looks—the definition of a `wrapper` function actually lies inside of `@ints_only`. So when `@ints_only` is called, it defines and then returns the `wrapper` function.

> Each time `@ints_only` is called, it defines a new `wrapper` function.

When a function is defined inside another function, the containing function's local variables remain available to the inner function. Refer to the following code example:

```
from functools import wraps

def ints_only(func):
    @wraps(func):
    def wrapper(*args, **kawrgs):
        args = [int(x) for x in args]
        kwargs = {n: int(v)
                    for n, v
                    in kwargs.items()}
        return func(*args, **kwargs)
    return wrapper

@ints_only
def add(left, right):
    return left + right

add('57', 99.5)
```

In the preceding case, the `wrapper` does some manipulation of the function arguments and then calls the wrapped function and returns its results. We imported and used the decorator called `@wraps` in the preceding example.

The `@wraps` decorator's job is pretty straightforward; it makes the wrapper look like a wrapped function for tools such as `pydoc`. However, `@wraps` takes a parameter.

How does it work if the decorator always accepts just one parameter and that's the function it's being applied to? Let's find out.

The @wraps decorator

The key is that the @ symbol isn't followed by the name of a decorator per se; it's followed by an expression that evaluates to a decorator. So, wraps isn't actually a decorator. Strictly speaking, it's a function that returns the decorator.

 When Python evaluates the function call expression, @wraps returns a decorator function, which is then applied to our wrapper.

The only function

If we were to modify our @ints_only decorator so that we could specify an arbitrary function that could be applied to all the parameters, it would look like the preceding example. So now we have a function called only, which returns a decorator, which in turn returns a wrapper. This wrapper calls the original function.

That might look terribly inefficient, but in fact the only overhead comes from invoking the wrapper. Each time we call the function, the outer two layers of code only run once when the function is defined. So that's how you use function decorators and taste the sort of things we can use them for.

Function annotations

In this section, we'll take a look at how to associate metadata with functions beyond docstrings, which we discussed in Chapter 4, *Basic Best Practices*. In the previous section, one of our examples was a decorator that automatically passed all our decorated function arguments through an adapter.

That's pretty cool, but what if we want to handle each parameter differently?

Sure, we could pass a whole bunch of adapters to the wrapper, but it becomes ugly and clumsy as we start dealing with functions that accept more parameters. What we'd really like to do is attach metadata directly to a function's parameters. Fortunately, that's exactly what function annotations are for.

Function annotation syntax

The following code example shows off Python's function annotation syntax:

```
>>> def foo(a: int, b: float) -> bool:
...     pass
...
```

To associate a value with a parameter, we put a colon (:) after the parameter name and then write an expression. This expression will be evaluated when the function is defined and the result stored along with a parameter name.

We can also annotate the return value of a function by writing a -> arrow symbol after the function's parameter list and then an expression, which will also be evaluated when the function is defined. The result is stored along with the word return. Because return is a keyword, there is no chance that it will collide with a parameter name.

Accessing annotation data

All the annotations are stored in a dictionary called __annotations__, which is an attribute of the function itself:

```
>>> foo.__annotations__
{'return': <class 'bool'>, 'b': <class 'float'>, 'a': <class 'int'>}
>>>
```

As we can see in the preceding code example, annotations are not type declarations, though they could certainly be used for that purpose and they resemble the typing syntax used in some other languages, as shown here:

```
>>> def foo(a: 'aardvark', b: {'stuff:' 'rocks'}) -> 'yo':
...     pass
...
>>> foo.__annotations__
{'return': 'yo', 'b': {'stuff:rocks'}, 'a': 'aardvark'}
>>>
```

They are arbitrary expressions, which means that arbitrary values can be stored in the __annotations__ dictionary. They don't add any meaning to Python itself, except that it should store the values. That said, defining parameter and return types is a common use of function annotations.

The @no_type_check decorator

If you find yourselves using a tool that assumes annotations are type declarations but you want to use them for some other purpose, use the standard `@no_type_check` decorator to exempt your function from such processing, as shown here:

```
>>> from typing import no_type_check
>>> @no_type_check
... def foo(a: 'aardvark', b: {'stuff:' 'rocks'}) -> 'yo':
...     pass
...
>>>
```

Normally, this isn't needed because most tools that use annotations have a way of recognizing the ones meant for them. The decorator is for protecting corner cases where things are ambiguous.

Annotations as input to function decorators

Annotations combine well with decorators because annotation values make a good way to provide input to a decorator, and decorator-generated wrappers are a good place to put code that gives meaning to annotations.

For example, let's rewrite the decorator example from the previous section. We'll switch to only accepting keyword arguments, just to keep the example relatively simple:

```
from functools import wraps

def adapted(func):
    @wraps(func)
    def wrapper(**kwargs):
        final_args = {}

        for name, value in kwargs.items():
            adapt = func.__annotations__.get(name)
            if adapt is not None:
                final_args[name] = adapt(value)
            else:
                final_args[name] = value

        result = func(**final_args)

        adapt = func.__annotations__.get('return')
        if adapt is not None:
            return adapt(result)
        return result

    return wrapper

@adapted
def foo(a : int, b : repr) -> str:
    return a
```

So, the `adapted` decorator encloses the function in a `wrapper`. This `wrapper` only accepts keyword arguments, which means that even, if the original function could accept positional arguments, they have to be specified by name.

Once the function is wrapped, `wrapper` also looks for adapters in the function's parameter annotations and applies them before passing the arguments to the real function.

Once the function returns, the wrapper checks for a return value adapter; if it finds one, it applies it to the return value before finally returning it.

When we consider the implications of what's happening here, they're pretty impressive. We've actually modified what it means to pass a parameter to a function or return a value.

Keyword arguments

Let's look at another example (refer to the following example). Sometimes, one or more of a method's parameters don't require any processing, except assigning them to an attribute of self. Can we use decorators and annotations to make this happen automatically? Of course we can.

```python
from functools import wraps

def store_args(func):
    @wraps(func)
    def wrapper(self, **kwargs):
        for name, value in kwargs.items():
            attrib = func.__annotations__.get(name)
            if attrib is True:
                attrib = name
            if isinstance(attrib, str):
                setattr(self, attrib, value)
        return func(self, **kwargs)
    return wrapper

class A:
    @store_args
    def __init__(self, first: True, second: 'example'):
        pass

a = A(first = 5, second = 6)
assert a.first == 5
assert a.example == 6
```

Let's say that if a parameter is annotated with a string, the value assigned to that parameter will be assigned to an attribute of self, using the string as the name. And if the parameter is annotated with true, the attribute will have the same name as the parameter. If there's no annotation or, if it's not a string or true, nothing will happen.

Again, for simplicity's sake, let's limit ourselves to keyword arguments. As you can see in the preceding example, annotations simplify all sorts of code base manipulations of code. Here, we're basically using the same techniques as in the previous example but we're doing something entirely different with them.

We've been looking at decorators as the primary consumers of function annotations, but that's not necessarily the case. Any code that uses function objects might be written to benefit from annotations. This means, anywhere we pass a function as a callback, we could potentially use function annotation data to make the code smarter about what it does with the function.

Some of the possibilities are presented in the following list:

- Event handlers could be annotated with the names of the values the handler wants to receive
- Dependency injection could be automated in a similar way
- Constraint-based systems could be provided with the constraints that could be applied to each parameter
- Probabilistic reasoning systems could be annotated with prior probability distributions
- Parameters could be annotated with the proper user interface element to display in order to have the user input that parameter's value

Inspecting the package signature function

Before we wrap up this section, I'd like to point out one thing that may be helpful down the road. Our example decorators that worked with annotations were all limited to keyword arguments for simplicity:

```
>>> from inspect import signature
>>> signature(foo)
<Signature (a:'aardvark', b:{'stuff:rocks'}) -> 'yo'>
>>>
```

However, if you find yourself wanting to do similar things and also handle all sorts of parameters at the same time, the `inspect` package's `signature` function will simplify the process significantly.

So, function annotations are a great way of adding metadata to functions; however, they might affect the handling of functions later in all sorts of ways.

Class decorators

In this section, we'll look at class decorators, which are conceptually similar to function decorators but open different doors.

Class decorators work in the same basic way that function decorators do. A class decorator receives the class as its only parameter, and whatever it returns replaces that class. This is illustrated in the following image:

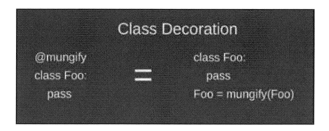

The return value doesn't have to be the same class or even a class at all, but it should be something that is meaningful. When it's bound to the class's name, it's rarely useful for a decorator to return none.

Also, like a function decorator, a class decorator can modify the attributes of the class or enclose the whole class in wrapper code. However, modifying the attributes of the class is effectively the same as modifying the class of the source code. This means that unlike functions, a class decorator can actually alter the structure of the decorated code, not just wrap it.

Modifying class attributes

Modifying class attributes is straightforward; we just use the built-in `getattr`, `setattr`, and `delattr` functions, as shown in the following code example:

```
def attritems(class_):
    def _getitem(self, key):
        return getattr(self, key)

    setattr(class_, '__getitem__', _getitem)

    if getattr(class_, '__setitem__', None):
        delattr(class_, '__setitem__')

    if getattr(class_, '__delitem__', None):
        delattr(class_, '__delitem__')

    return class_

@attritems
class Foo:
    def __init__(self):
        self.a = 'hello'
        self.b = 'world'

f = Foo()

assert f['a'] == 'hello'
assert f['b'] == 'world'
```

In the preceding example, we see a simple class decorator that makes the attributes of the decorated class readable through the `[]` syntax; at the same time, it makes sure the class doesn't allow you to set or delete values through the `[]` syntax. While rewriting classes via decorators can be a powerful technique, it's not a complicated or surprising task, so there's nothing much to say about it.

We can also wrap up classes in their entirety. One common use of this technique is that it helps replace a class with a `factory` function. Using a `factory` function as an interface to create class instances lets us choose when to return an existing object, if there's one interface we think is more appropriate, rather than actually creating a new instance.

The factory function

Calling a `factory` function means *give me the right object for these parameters, rather than giving me a new object for these parameters*. Let's take a look at an example class decorator that replaces the class object with a factory function.

For instances of this class, we'll assume that any two instances that were created with the same parameters should actually be the same object, as shown here:

```
from weakref import WeakValueDictionary

def factory_constructed(class_):
    cache = WeakValueDictionary()

    def factory(*args, **kwargs):
        key = (args, frozenset(kwargs.items()))
        instance = cache.get(key)
        if instance is not None:
            return instance
        instance = class_(*args, **kwargs)
        cache[key] = instance
        return instance

    factory.type = class_

    return factory
```

In the preceding example, we used `WeakValueDictionary` to keep track of the existing instances of the class and what parameters that were constructed with.

This doesn't have anything to do with class decorators per se; instead, we did it because we didn't want the cache to prevent the instances from being garbage collected. That's a good practice!

Whenever we make a `factory` function, it keeps track of the instances it creates. Another bit of good practice that we demonstrated in this example is that we decide the class itself as an attribute of the `factory` function. This means that the code outside of the `factory` function can still access the class object if it really needs to.

The factory_constructed function

So, let's take a look at our factory-making decorator in action. Refer to the following screenshot:

```
>>> from factory import factory_constructed
>>> @factory_constructed
... class Unique:
...     def __init__(self, *words):
...         self.words = words
...
>>> Unique
<function factory_constructed.<locals>.factory at 0x7f5311c97bf8>
>>> Unique.type
<class '__main__.Unique'>
>>> u1 = Unique('hello', 'world')
>>> u2 = Unique('hello', 'Oklahoma')
>>> u3 = Unique('hello', 'world')
>>> u1 is i2
Traceback (most recent call last):
  File "<stdin>", line 1, in <module>
NameError: name 'i2' is not defined
>>> u1 is u2
False
>>> u1 is u3
True
>>>
```

Notice that the thing named Unique is in fact the factory function that was created for the Unique class, rather than the Unique class itself. The actual class ends up being named Unique.type. Also, notice that u1 and u3 are not just equal but actually the same object; meanwhile, u2, which was created with different arguments, is different.

Class definitions

Now we're going to take a look at something really wild. The syntax we use for defining classes is pretty generic; it could be used to represent all sorts of different data structures. So, why not use class decorators to transform class definitions into objects of various types?

By doing this, we can achieve a sort of sideways decorative programming paradigm. For our example (the one that will follow), let's say we want to connect to a sqlite database and create some tables in it if they don't already exist. We can make Python's class syntax work for us as a convenient way of expressing this idea:

```
>>> from database import database
>>> @database
... class db:
...     class Table1:
...         name = 'TEXT'
...         age = 'INTEGER'
...     class Table2:
...         alpha = 'INTEGER'
...         beta = 'INTEGER'
...
>>> db.execute('INSERT INTO Table1 (name, age) VALUES ("Alice", 25)')
<sqlite3.Cursor object at 0x7f5311c7b420>
>>>
```

We want the usage to look something like this code example, where the class structure and attributes provide the information that's needed to construct and configure a database connection for us. The end result should be a connection object, which we can use to issue queries according to the Python Database API.

There are a great many details that are ignored or handled simplistically by this example, but it captures the general idea. The class objects that Python creates automatically, when it's evaluating these statements, are used to provide structured data input to the decorator called @database and then discarded.

The following code example shows the @database decorator:

```
import sqlite3

def database(connclass):
    fname = getattr(connclass, 'database', 'default.sqlite')
    connection = sqlite3.connect(fname, detect_types=sqlite3.PARSE_DECLTYPES)

    for tablename in dir(connclass):
        if tablename.startswith('_'):
            continue

        tabledata = getattr(connclass, tablename, None)

        if not isinstance(tabledata, type):
            continue

        columns = []

        for colname in dir(tabledata):
            if colname.startswith('_'):
                continue
            coldata = getattr(tabledata, colname, None)
            if coldata in ('INTEGER', 'TEXT'):
                columns.append('{} {}'.format(colname, coldata))

        sql = 'CREATE TABLE IF NOT EXISTS {} ({});'
        sql = sql.format(tablename, ', '.join(columns))

        connection.execute(sql)

    return connection
```

The @database decorator returns an open Python Database API connection object, not a class of any sort.

Metaclasses

In this section, we'll look at metaclasses, which affect the creation of class objects right from the beginning.

Like class decorators, metaclasses are a tool we can use to adjust the basic meaning of a class. In concept though, they're very different. A class decorator takes an already created class and transforms it in some way. A metaclass, on the other hand, can affect how a class is created, how it behaves, and even how classes that inherit from the modified class are created and behave.

To understand metaclasses, first we have to grasp the idea that classes are objects, and more than that, they are instances of another class called `type`. Whenever we create a new class, we create an instance of `type`, unless the class has a metaclass, as shown here:

```
>>> class ExampleMeta (type):
...     @staticmethod
...     def __prepare__(name, bases, **kwargs):
...         return dict()
...
>>> from collections import OrderedDict
>>> class ExampleMeta (type):
...     @staticmethod
...     def __prepare__(name, bases, **kwargs):
...         return orderedDict()
...
>>>
```

If the class we're creating as a metaclass is specified or inherits a metaclass from its ancestors, then the new class is an instance of the metaclass rather than a direct instance of `type`.

This sounds like we could change the behavior of a class completely by giving it an unusual metaclass, but actually all metaclasses have to resemble `type` or Python wouldn't be able to use them properly. Most of the time, metaclasses are actually subclasses of `type`, which makes things simple.

What can we do with a metaclass?

First of all, we can run code before the code inside the `class` block is evaluated for each class, which is an instance of the metaclass. We do this by having the metaclass set as a `__prepare__` method, which should be a class method or a static method because it will be called before the instance is created.

The __prepare__ method

The `__prepare__` method is passed with the name of the new class and its list of parent classes as well as any keyword arguments supplied by the user. It can do whatever we want it to, but it should also return a dictionary or similar object that could be used to hold the class's attributes (refer to the previous example).

We can preassign values to the attribute dictionary from inside of __prepare__, so we can actually assign attributes to the class before it even exists. That brings us to the second thing that metaclasses can easily control-the **class's namespace**.

In our previous example, we returned a dict() instance from __prepare__, so instances of this metaclass use a normal dictionary to store their attributes while their code is being evaluated; however, we can return any dictionary-like object from __prepare__. For example, we can return OrderedDict if we want to keep track of the order in which attributes were created or DefaultDict if we want all the attributes to have a default value.

 We could even use WeakValueDictionary if, for some reason, we want the class to not protect its attributes from being garbage collected while it is evaluated. Of course, WeakValueDictionary is a just dictionary-like class that exists in the standard library.

We can also return a custom dictionary-like class from __prepare__, which could conceivably do almost anything. If we want a class that ignores the case of attribute names while its code is being evaluated, we can do that.

The __new__ method

There's a reason why I keep saying *while the code is being evaluated*. After __prepare__ is called, the code inside the class block is run and it uses the dictionary that was returned from __prepare__ as its namespace, as shown here:

```
>>> from collections import OrderedDict
>>> class ExampleMeta (type):
...     @staticmethod
...     def __prepare__ (name, bases, **kwargs):
...         return OrderedDict()
...     def __new__ (metaclass, name, bases, namespace, **kwargs):
...         class_ = type.__new__(metaclass, name, bases, namespace)
...         class_.order = tuple(namespace.keys())
...         return class_
...
>>> class Foo(metaclass = ExampleMeta):
...     z = 7
...     a = 2
...     m = 90
...
>>> Foo.order
('__module__', '__qualname__', 'z', 'a', 'm')
>>>
```

However, after that, the metaclass's __new__ method is called. One of the things __new__ needs to do is call type.__new__ to actually allocate and initialize a chunk of memory to contain the class data, and one of the things type.__new__ does is convert whatever we pass as a namespace for the object into a normal dict.

This means that if we want to retain special information that our namespace object knows, we need to store it somewhere where we can find it later.

We can make whatever changes we want to the internals of the class, shown in the following code example:

```
class RegisterDescendants(type):
    def __new__(cls, name, bases, namespace, **kwargs):
        class_ = type.__new__(cls, name, bases, namespace)
        registry = getattr(class_, 'REGISTRY', set())
        registry.add(class_)
        setattr(class_, 'REGISTRY', registry)
        return class_
```

Once we've created the class object in the __new__ method of the metaclass, we can programmatically add, remove, replace, or wrap the class contents, much as we could in a class decorator. We can also return something that isn't actually a class object at all, just as we could with a class decorator.

The difference, aside from a bit of extra typing, is that the subclasses of a class that has a metaclass will also inherit that metaclass, while class decorators are not inherited.

 This means that using a metaclass, we can make our unusual behaviors inheritable.

In this example, you learned that any class that descends from the class where the metaclass was originally applied can find all the other classes that also descend from that ancestor.

Context managers

In this section, we'll look at what is maybe Python's most-used programmable semantic element—context managers.

Context managers are pieces of code that plug into Python's `with` statement. A `with` statement contains a block of code, and the context manager is able to run its own code, both before and after that block is executed, along with the after code guaranteed to run no matter what happens in the block.

The Python standard library makes quite a lot of use of context managers:

- `open` files can be used as context managers, which guarantees that the file will be closed at the end of the block:

```
>>> with open('example.txt', 'w') as f:
...     f.write('Hello world\n')
...
12
>>>
```

- `lock` objects could be used as context managers, in which case they acquire the lock before the block and release it when the block is finished executing:

```
>>> import multiprocessing
>>> man = multiprocessing.Manager()
>>> lock = man.Lock()
>>> with lock:
...    print('The lock is acquired, and will be released at the end of this block')
...
The lock is acquired, and will be released at the end of this block
>>>
```

- SQLite database connections can be used as context managers, allowing them to automatically commit or roll back the transaction when the block finishes:

```
>>> import sqlite3
>>> con = sqlite3.connect(':memory')
>>> with con:
...     con.execute('CREATE TABLE example (x INTEGER, y INTEGER)')
...
<sqlite3.Cursor object at 0x7f530eed4340>
>>>
```

There are other examples. We can already see in the preceding examples how useful context managers can be. They simplify the code by combining setup and cleanup, and they improve the code by guaranteeing that they will run the cleanup code.

Defining a context manager as a generator

So how can we write our own context managers? There are two ways.

The simplest is to use the @contextlib.contextmanager decorator on a generator function, as we see in the following example:

```
>>> import contextlib
>>> @contextlib.contextmanager
... def before_and_after():
...     print('before')
...     try:
...         yield(lambda: print('during'))
...     finally:
...         print('after')
...
>>> with before_and_after() as during:
...     print('When I call during(), I get:')
...     during()
...
before
When I call during(), I get:
during
after
>>>
```

When we create a context manager this way, we can write it as one continuous piece of code. We can think of the yield statement as a proxy for the whole code block that the with statement contains.

If this block raises an exception, it will look toward our context manager code as if the yield statement was responsible for raising that exception, so we can wrap it in a try statement to deal with any exceptions that might occur.

We saw the as clause of the with statement when we used file opening as an example of a context manager (refer to the code example of the open file); it lets us find a value returned from the context manager to a variable accessible within the with block. If we yield a value from our context manager code, that value will be the one assigned through as.

In the preceding example, we yield a function that prints the word during so that the entire result of our with statement is that it prints before, during, and after, in that order.

Adding context manager behavior to a class

We can also write context managers by adding __enter__ and __exit__ methods to objects. Any object that properly implements these methods can be used as a context manager, which is how objects such as open files and database connections are able to work extra as context managers.

Synchronous-coroutine-based context managers

The following is an example in which we create a specialized version of a dictionary, which could serve as a context manager:

```python
from collections import ChainMap

class TransactionDict(dict):
    def __enter__(self):
        self.writes = dict()
        return ChainMap(self.writes, self)

    def __exit__(self, exc_type, exc_val, tb):
        if exc_type is None:
            self.update(self.writes)
        self.writes = None
```

Within the scope of the with block, we can read and write data through the object that we returned from __enter__, but these changes will only be applied to the main dictionary. If the block exits without raising an exception, the return value of the inner method will be used by the with statement for the value to be assigned through the as clause.

Refer to the following code example, the variable `trans` contains the `ChainMap` instance. `ChainMap` objects are dictionaries that can have a parent dictionary. If `'a'` looking in `ChainMap` fails, it tries to look up the same key in its parent.

```
from collections import ChainMap

class TransactionDict(dict):
    def __enter__(self):
        self.writes = dict()
        return ChainMap(self.writes, self)

    def __exit__(self, exc_type, exc_val, tb):
        if exc_type is None:
            self.update(self.writes)
        self.writes = None

if __name__ == '__main__':
    tdict = TransactionDict()
    with tdict as trans:
        trans['a'] = 1
```

The `__exit__` method needs to accept parameters that specify the types `exc_type`, `exc_val`, and `tb`, if an exception is raised in the `with` block. If no exception is raised, all these parameters will contain `None`. If an exception is raised, we would need to decide whether and how the context manager will handle them.

In our preceding example, we decided to apply the changes to the main dictionary based on whether or not an exception was raised; otherwise, we would have ignored the exception. If we want Python to consider the exception to be handled, we could return `true` from the `__exit__` method.

This would be functionally equivalent to catching the function with a `try-except` statement. There's another variation of the class-based context manager, which supports asynchronous-coroutine-based context management.

Creating an asynchronous-coroutine-based context manager

For the asynchronous protocol, the __enter__ and __exit__ methods are replaced by __aenter__ and __aexit__ coroutine methods and the context manager is invoked by an async with statement, as shown here:

```python
from collections import ChainMap

class AsyncTransactionDict(dict):
    async def __aenter__(self):
        self.writes = dict()
        return ChainMap(self.writes, self)

    async def __aexit__(self, exc_type, exc_val, tb):
        if exc_type is None:
            self.update(self.writes)
        self.writes = None
```

This small change buys us the ability to have the __enter__ and __exit__ methods invoke other coroutines, wait for data to come in from the network, and behave nicely in an asyncio-based program.

Descriptors

In this section, we'll take a look at one last way of altering the semantics of a Python-based syntax, using descriptors. Reading and writing variables is one of the most fundamental aspects of programming. Python's descriptors let us alter how it works.

A descriptor is an object that is stored in a class and controls what it means to get, set, and delete a specific single attribute for instances of that class. If we want that sort of control over multiple attributes, we just add a descriptor to the class for each attribute we want to control.

Using @property to create a descriptor

Python's built-in `@property` decorator provides a simple way to create a descriptor. Let's consider an example (refer to the following code example) to illustrate this:

```
>>> class HasProperty:
...     @property
...     def prop(self):
...         val = self._prop
...         print ('getter produces', val)
...         return val
...     @prop.setter
...     def prop(self, value):
...         self._prop = value
...         print('setter received', value)
...     @prop.deleter
...     def prop(self):
...         del self._prop
...         print('deleted')
...
>>>
```

The first `prop` method we wrote in the preceding code example tells Python how to figure out the value of an attribute called `prop`, which in this case just means fetching it from another attribute and printing the value.

The latter two `prop` methods are decorated to turn them into `setter` and `deleter` for the `prop` attribute. This means that assigning a value to a prop actually means calling the `setter` method, and deleting a prop attribute actually means calling the `deleter` method.

Both the methods are optional for properties. Leaving them out makes the attribute that the property describes into a read-only attribute.

Writing descriptors as classes

Properties simplify the construction of descriptors for a common case, but there are use cases where we need a descriptor that the property can't handle well. For example, what if we were planning on making a class that represented remote data and we wanted its attributes to push and pull data from a remote source? We could do this with properties, but we'd end up writing very similar code over and over as we implement each attribute.

It would be better to have a `RemoteResource` descriptor class and just add a bunch of instances to our local stub class. Let's go ahead and do that as an example using the `RemoteResource` descriptor; refer to the following code example:

```python
import asyncio

class RemoteResource:
    def __init__(self, name):
        self.name = name

    def to_str(self, val):
        return str(val)

    def from_str(self, val):
        return val

    async def _fetcher(self, instance, name, future):
        out = instance.out
        in_ = instance.in_
        pk = instance.pk
        out.write('fetch {} {}\n'.format(pk, name))
        value = await in_.readline()
        future.set_result(self.from_str(value))

    def __get__(self, instance, class_):
        if instance is None:
            return self
        future = asyncio.Future()
        coro = self._fetcher(instance, self.name, future)
        asyncio.ensure_future(coro)
        return future

    def __set__(self, instance, value):
        pk = instance.pk
        name = self.name
        value = self.to_str(value)
        template = 'set {} {}\n{}\n'
        command = template.format(pk, name, value)
        instance.out.write(command)

    def __delete__(self, instance):
        pk = instance.pk
        name = self.name
        command = 'delete {} {}\n'.format(pk, name)
        instance.out.write(command)

class RemoteInt(RemoteResource):
    def from_string(self, value):
        return int(value)

class Record:
    name = RemoteResource('name')
    age = RemoteInt('age')

    def __init__(self, pk, reader, writer):
        self.out = writer
        self.in_ = reader
        self.pk = pk
```

 Actually, interacting with the network requires a fair amount of code, so it's a good thing we can avoid repeating it over and over.

The `RemoteResource` class we have in the preceding example has __get__, __set__, and __delete__ methods, which determine what happens when an attribute that is controlled by an instance in this class is accessed.

- The __get__ method, perhaps surprisingly, takes two parameters-the `instance` through which the attribute's being accessed and the `class` through which the attribute is being accessed. It's like this so we can handle both `instance` attribute access and `class` attribute access.
  - When accessing a `class` attribute, the `instance` parameter is `None`. In our case, we just returned the descriptor in case somebody tries to access the attribute as a class member instead of an instance member, which is a reasonable default in a lot of cases.

- The __set__ method is passed as an instance and value, and it conceptually represents setting the control attribute of that instance to the value. Unlike __get__, it doesn't have support for setting a `class` attribute, so the instance will never be `None` and we don't need `class_parameter`.
- The __delete__ method is just passed as an instance and represents removing the control attribute from that instance.

> None of the descriptor methods are told which attribute they represent. The assumption is that their `self` parameter will specify that one way or another.

In our code (in the preceding code example), we've chosen to pass the necessary information to the descriptor's constructor and store it as an attribute of self. But, in other circumstances, we might use `self` or `selfs ID` as a key in a dictionary to store the per-instance state of the descriptor or use the instance as a key in a dictionary stored in `self` as shown in the following code example:

```
class Record:
    name = RemoteResource('name')
    age = RemoteInt('age')
    def __init__(self, pk, reader, writer):
        self.out = writer
        self.in = reader
        self.pk = pk
```

We can't just store per-instance data as attributes of `self`, though. Descriptors are attributes of the class, not the instance, so their self values are shared by all the instances of the class that contains them. Either way, we can control what it means to get, set, or delete an instance attribute.

Once we have the `RemoteResource` class, creating classes that have remote attributes becomes easy, as demonstrated by the `Record` class shown in the preceding image.

Summary

In this chapter, we saw several other ways of altering the meaning and execution of Python code, allowing us to conform the language to our specialized needs.

We saw how function decorators use functions as input data for manipulation. We took a look at function annotations and particularly how they interact with function decorators. We saw how class decorators work exactly as function decorators do, but because they operate on classes, the possibilities are very different. We saw how to modify classes, wrap them, or even replace them using decorators. We discussed how to use a metaclass to affect the construction of a class object and how to make unusual behavior inheritable by making it part of a class's metaclass. We looked at context manager, both synchronous and asynchronous. We saw how context managers work and learned how to make our own for use in either synchronous or asynchronous code. We saw how to create simple descriptors using the `property` function and more complex descriptors as classes.

In the next chapter, we'll look at automated unit testing—testing a set of techniques that could dramatically improve the process of writing a program.

9
Unit Testing

In the previous chapter, we saw various approaches to metaprogramming and programmable syntax in Python. In this chapter, we're going to take a look at the ideas behind unit testing, then move on to several test automation tools we can use to make our testing easier and more useful. We'll focus on what unit testing is, and the ideas that motivate it. We'll also discuss Python's standard `unittest` package and how it works.

Finally, you'll learn how to use `unittest.mock` to control the environment that your test code will run in so that the test will remain focused on making sure one thing works properly.

In this chapter, we'll cover the following topics:

- Understanding the principle of unit testing
- Using the unittest package
- Using unittest.mock
- Using unittest's test discovery
- Using nose for unified test discovery and reporting

Understanding the principle of unit testing

Testing is often something of an afterthought for programmers because it tends to be laborious and annoying. Also, we usually have a high degree of confidence in our work and testing it seems unnecessary. It's also a fact, though, that the confidence is often misplaced. Source code is a complex and subtle language, and it's easy to make mistakes while writing it and not even notice them. We all know this from experience, but that doesn't make it any easier to make time for something that is laborious, annoying, and feels unnecessary. The following flow diagram illustrates a simple example of testing:

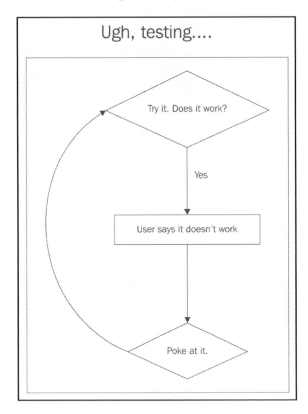

So, the first question about testing is, *How can we do it in a way that doesn't feel like a painful waste of time?* Finding a way to overcome this psychological barrier is the first step toward creating a testing method that will actually work for a lot of programmers. Unit testing does this by reducing the effort needed to run tests, integrating testing with the development process, and making the tests themselves visibly useful.

What is a unit test?

First of all, let's find out what is a unit test. A **unit test** is a single small chunk of test code that tests correct behavior or a single specific flaw within an isolated small chunk of program code.

There are reasons for each part of this definition. A unit test is source code because one of the secrets of unit testing is that we put the maximum amount of the effort of testing on the computer, which is where it should belong.

The test code tells the computer how to perform the test, which allows us to perform the test often and easily. A unit test is small because a large test is almost inevitably testing for more than one thing.

This can be summarized as:

- Small, simple code
- Checks a small piece of the program
- Answers a single yes-or-no question about program functionality

> If we want to test for more than one thing, we should write more than one test.

There are two rules for a unit test. These are:

- A unit test only checks a single aspect of the program code because when a test fails, we want it to tell us exactly what the problem is
- A unit test only involves a narrow region of the program code because when a test fails, we want it to tell us exactly where the problem is

If we write a collection of tests that follow these rules, they are called a **unit test suite**.

With proper tools, we can run our whole test suite with a single command, and the output of this command will immediately tell us the status of our code with respect to the test. If the test fails, it tells us what we need to work on next. If it succeeds, it gives us a reason to build our confidence in the code it tested.

The availability of automated unit testing leads to a programming paradigm called **test-driven development** (**TDD**), as illustrated in the following diagram:

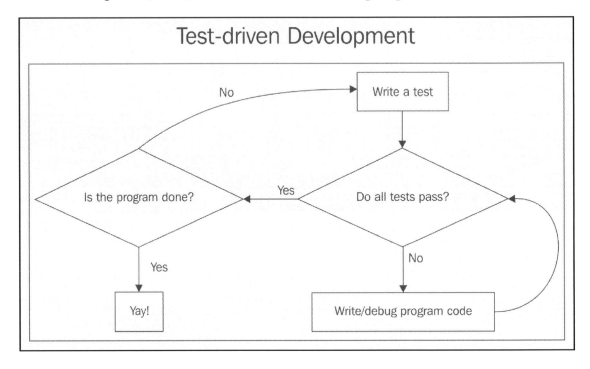

The basic idea of TDD is that since a failing test tells us what to do next, we should never write program code except when we want to make a failing test pass. If all the presently available tests pass and the program isn't finished, we first add another test to the test suite, and then write program code to make it pass.

Doing things this way ensures that there are tests that cover most or all of the source code and that the tests are run often, which makes it very difficult for bugs and regressions to sneak into the code without being noticed. It also lets us break the development process down into a series of short-term goals, which produce a visible result when we achieve them.

 This is psychologically useful because it makes the programming process feel more productive, and it's much easier to perform a task that feels rewarding. Further, debugging tends to dominate the time needed for a project, and TDD reduces the time needed to deal with bugs.

So, when applied properly, unit testing principles and tools help us produce better code, perform the test faster, and enjoy the process more. It's an all-round win.

So far, we've had a high-level discussion of the reasons for and the benefits of automated unit testing and TDD. Python includes a framework for automated unit testing, and we'll take a look at it in the next section.

Using the unittest package

In this section, we're going to look at Python's standard unittest package. We'll talk about how to structure a test file and how to write tests and draw a comparison between what happens and what should happen in these tests. Let's jump straight into it!

Structuring a test file

The unittest module contains a framework for performing automated unit testing. Most of this functionality is based around the unittest.TestCase class, which we will inherit from to create our own tests.

In the following example, we see the basic features of TestCase in action and also test and assert methods:

```
import unittest

class BasicTest(unittest.TestCase):
    def test_addition(self):
        self.assertEqual(2 + 2, 4)
```

Any method that we define using a class inherited from TestCase, and that has a name that starts with the word **test**, is assumed to be a unit test. In the preceding example, this means that the test_addition method is a unit test; however, if we had added another method to the class, called connect, the unittest module would not have treated it as a unit test.

A TestCase class can contain more than one unit test and should run when those tests are logically related and require the same operating environment.

assert methods

Inside our `test_addition` method, which is a unit test, we used a method called `assertEqual` to actually check that the result of the code was as expected. `TestCase` provides a wide range of these assert methods that test for various relationships between our results and what we expected. This is shown in the following code example:

```
>>> import unittest
>>> class Operators(unittest.TestCase):
...     def test_operators(self):
...         self.assertEqual(5, 5)
...         self.assertnotEqual(5, 7)
...         #
...         self.assertGreaterEqual(5, 5)
...         self.assertGreater(5, 3)
...         self.assertLess(3, 5)
...         self.assertLessEqual(5, 5)
...         #
...         self.assertTrue(True)
...         self.assertFalse(False)
...         #
...         self.assertIs(None, None)
...         self.assertIsNot(5, None)
...         self.assertIsNone(None)
...         self.assertIsNotNone(5)
...         #
...         self.assertInstance(5, int)
...         self.assertIsNotInstance(5, str)
...         #
...         self.assertIn(5, (3, 5, 7))
...         self.assertNotIn(5, (2, 4, 6))
...         self.assertCountEqual((1, 2, 3, 3), (3, 2, 3, 1))
...         #
...         with self.assertRaises(ValueError):
...             raise ValueError
...
```

Let's take a closer look at what these assert methods actually do:

- We've already seen the `assertEqual` method in the previous code example; it checks whether two values are equal and makes the test fail if they are not. The `assertNotEqual` method performs the inverse operation, checking whether two values are equal and failing the test if they are.

- The `assertAlmostEqual` and `assertNotAlmostEqual` methods are for use with floating point numbers.

  The way computers handle floating point numbers indicates that numbers that should be exactly equal actually differ in their least significant bits. For example, if we square the square root of seven, the result is not exactly seven, so `assertEqual` will treat it as *not equal*. However, `assertAlmostEqual` will recognize that the two numbers are the same for practical purposes.

- The `assertGreaterEqual`, `assertLess`, and `assertLessEqual` methods check for ordering relationships between their arguments.
- The `assertIs` and `assertIsNot` methods check whether their arguments are references to the exact same object.
- The `assertIsNone` and `assertIsNotNone` methods are a special case of `assertIs` and `assertIsNot` methods and check whether their single argument is in fact `None`.
- The `assertIsInstance` and `assertIsNotInstant` methods check whether the object in the first argument is an instance of the type in their second argument.
- The `assertIn` and `assertNotIn` check whether the object in the first argument is a member of the container in their second argument.
- The `assertCountEqual` method is interesting. If we want to check whether two sequences are the same, we could just use `assertEqual`, but `assertCountEqual` is for when we want to check whether two sequences contain the same values but don't care about the order.

  The method will cause a test to fail if any of the members of either sequence appears in the other sequence a different number of times. So, if a is in the first sequence twice, it has to be in the second sequence twice as well, but we don't care where.

- Finally, we have `assertRaises`, which functions a little differently because it needs to catch the exception raised by running some code. This is a situation tailor-made for a context manager, and that's what `assertRaises` is.

Used in a `with` statement, `assertRaises` makes the test fail if the code inside the with block does not raise the expected exception. This could seem a little backward, but it's correct. The test fails if the expected exception is not raised. Sometimes, raising an exception is the correct behavior. For example, passing `None` to the end constructor should raise a type error, and if it doesn't, that's a bug.

Comparing what happens to what should happen in unit tests

I mentioned in passing that all the unit tests in a `TestCase` class should share the same operating environment. What does that mean?

It means that each of them expects any external data that they access to be in the same state. For example, each of the tests accesses a particular file and each of them expects to find the same information inside that file.

Let's have a look at a code example:

```python
class SharedEnv(unittest.TestCase):
    def setUp(self):
        with open('test.txt', 'w') as f:
            f.write('a\nb\n')

    def tearDown(self):
        os.unlink('test.txt')

    def test_append(self):
        with open('test.txt', 'r') as f:
            lines = f.read().splitlines()

        self.assertEqual(lines, ['a', 'b'])

        lines.append('c')

        with open('test.txt', 'w') as f:
            f.write('\n'.join(lines))

    def test_replace(self):
        with open('test.txt', 'r') as f:
            lines = f.read().splitlines()

        self.assertEqual(lines, ['a', 'b'])

        lines[0] = 'q'

        with open('test.txt', 'w') as f:
            f.write('\n'.join(lines))
```

In the preceding example, we have two tests that both read and write in the same text file. Both of them expected to come in to contain the same specific information when they started running. In other words, both of them have the same expectations about their operating environment.

When we have multiple tests that share the same expectations and they're logically related, we should group them into a single `TestCase` class. Then, we should give that class a `setUp` method, which would be responsible for making sure those shared expectations are met, and possibly a `tearDown` method, which would clean up any changes that `setup` may have made or the tests left lying around.

 The name of the class itself doesn't matter; simply inheriting from `TestCase` is sufficient to identify them.

The `setUp` method is run before each unit test in `TestCase`. So, in our code example, which has two unit tests, `setUp` is run twice. Similarly, `tearDown` runs after each unit test. That way, the changes that one test might make to the operating environment are removed before the next test is run.

The starting environment is the same for each unit test in `TestCase`. So, that's the basic mechanics of Python's unit test framework, as far as writing tests goes.

To run the tests, we just need to invoke the `unittest` package from the command line. We tell it the name of the module we want to run the tests from and it finds the `TestCase` classes in that module, creates instances of them, runs all their tests, and gives us a report on which test has passed and which failed.

In this section, we've seen how to write basic unit tests and run them. There are even easier ways to run a test, but we'll look at them after we examine unit test mock objects.

Using unittest.mock

In this section, we'll take a look at a subpackage of unit tests, called **mock**. The tools in the `mock` package help us keep our test isolated, so they aren't made to succeed or fail based on the behavior of the code, which isn't supposed to be covered by the test.

We talked about how important it is that unit tests only interact with a small section of code, but how can we arrange for this when so many pieces of code interact with objects and functions originating from all over the source tree? One answer is that we can replace those objects and functions with mock objects.

What is a mock object?

A mock object is a clever piece of code; it could pretend to be almost any kind of object or function, but instead of doing whatever the original did, it just records what is done with it so we can check it later. Let's play with a mock object for a moment to get a feel for them:

```
>>> import unittest.mock
>>> m = unittest.mock.Mock()
>>> m.append('x')
<Mock name='mock.append()' id='140230015734168'>
>>> m.pop()
<Mock name='mock.pop()' id='140230015735008'>
>>> m.children.last()
<Mock name='mock.children.last()' id='140230015734784'>
>>>
```

Refer to the preceding screenshot. We can access pretty much any attribute of the mock object without defining it ahead of time. The result is another mock object. Similarly, we can call almost any method we want without defining it ahead of time and the result is yet another mock object, as shown here:

```
>>> m.method_calls
[call.append('x'), call.pop(), call.children.last()]
>>>
```

This by itself is enough to let a mock object replace a large range of functions and objects that our tested code might interact with. But, we can go further if we take time to preconfigure our mock objects.

Preconfiguring mock objects

We can assign non-mock objects to a mock object's attributes, so that when we access the attribute, we'd get a specific value instead of a generic mock object. This is illustrated by the following simple code example:

```
>>> m.foo = 5
>>> m.foo
5
>>>
```

We can also assign a customized mock object in place of a method so that we can make the mocked method act more like the original, but in a way, this is controlled by the test. We do this by passing a return value parameter to the mock constructor, which tells the mock object that every time it's called, it should return this value, as shown in the following code example:

```
>>> m.pop = unittest.mock.Mock(return_value= 'x')
>>> m.pop()
'x'
>>> m.pop()
'x'
>>>
```

If we want the mock to return different values each time it's called, we use a different parameter of the constructor, called side_effect, as shown next:

```
>>> from unittest.mock import Mock
>>> m = Mock(side_effect = [1, 2, 3])
>>> m()
1
>>> m()
2
>>> m()
3
>>>
```

We have to know how many times the test will call the mock as a function so we can provide a return value for each call; otherwise, this doesn't present a difficulty.

We can also make the mock object raise an exception by passing that exception as `side_effect` or a member of the `side_effect` sequence, as shown in the following code example:

```
>>> m = Mock(side_effect = TypeError('uh-oh'))
>>> m()
Traceback (most recent call last):
  File "<stdin>", line 1, in <module>
  File "/usr/lib/python3.5/unittest/mock.py", line 917, in __call__
    return _mock_self._mock_call(*args, **kwargs)
  File "/usr/lib/python3.5/unittest/mock.py", line 973, in _mock_call
    raise effect
TypeError: uh-oh
>>> m = Mock(side_effect = [1, TypeError('x')])
>>> m()
1
>>> m()
Traceback (most recent call last):
  File "<stdin>", line 1, in <module>
  File "/usr/lib/python3.5/unittest/mock.py", line 917, in __call__
    return _mock_self._mock_call(*args, **kwargs)
  File "/usr/lib/python3.5/unittest/mock.py", line 978, in _mock_call
    raise result
TypeError: x
>>>
```

That pretty well covers how to make a mock that can, in a controlled way, stand in for real objects and code while we run our test. However, to really support testing, we also need to be able to check the mock and confirm whether it was used as expected.

assert methods of mock objects

We've already seen the `method_calls` attribute that mock objects use to track their interactions, but mock objects also have their own assert methods that are usually easier to use than accessing the method calls' list directly.

The most useful mock object assertion method is `assert_called_with` (refer to the following code example):

```
>>> from unittest.mock import Mock
>>> m = Mock()
>>> m.bar(27)
<Mock name='mock.bar()' id='140230015736072'>
>>> m.bar(41)
<Mock name='mock.bar()' id='140230015736072'>
>>> m.bar.assert_called_with(41)
>>> m.bar.assert_any_call(27)
>>> m.bar.assert_called_with(27)
```

It checks whether the most recent call to the mock object was done with a specified argument and `assert_any_call`, which checks whether the mock has ever been called with specified arguments.

So, we know what mock objects are for, how to create them, and how to check the record of what has been done with them. That's enough for replacing the parameters of a tested function with mock objects.

We can even replace the `self` parameter of methods if we call the method via the class instead of a real instance:

```
>>> from unittest.mock import Mock
>>> class Example:
...     def foo(self, x):
...         self.x = x
...
>>> mock_self = Mock()
>>> Example.foo(mock_self, 5)
>>> mock_self.x
5
>>>
```

The unittest.mock patch function

What do we do, though, when the code we're testing reaches out to the system automatically and accesses something we want to replace with a mock object? For example, what if the code we're testing calls `time.time`? This is where the `unittest.mockpatch` function comes into play.

The `patch` function is a context manager and it could temporarily replace nearly any object in any package or module with a mock object. Once the with block exits, the real object is restored to its position, as shown in the following code example:

```
>>> from unittest.mock import patch
>>> with patch('time.time', return_value = 12):
...     import time
...     print(time.time())
...
12
>>>
```

Something to be aware of is that patch doesn't replace every reference to the target object with a mock; it only replaces the single reference that we specified in the first argument.

In the preceding example, any code that accesses the time function by looking up the reference in the `time` module will get our mock object; however, if there were any code that had used `from timeimport time` to create a local reference to the `time` function, then that reference would still refer to the real-time function. If we want to patch the time function for code that has a local reference to it, we need to pass the path to that local reference into the patch.

OK, we're pretty much good to go with mock objects now. This means we know everything we need to write powerful tests easily. All we are left to do is find out how to run our test suites, which is our next topic.

Using unittest's test discovery

In this section, we'll take a look at the `unittest` package's ability to run many tests at once with a single command.

We've seen how to easily run all the tests in a particular file, but for a large project, putting all the tests into a single file would be troublesome. They need to be separated into different files according to logical groupings, or the test suite will become unmanageable. On the other hand, it would be a pain to have to manually tell unittests to run the test and a whole bunch of files if we were to test or list out each file.

Fortunately, there's a way to split our test suites into many files and still run them with a simple command, as shown in the following code:

```
bhagya@bhagya-VirtualBox:~$ python3 -m unittest suite/test_one.py
.
----------------------------------------------------------------------
Ran 1 test in 0.000s

OK
bhagya@bhagya-VirtualBox:~$ python3 -m unittest suite/test_two.py
..
----------------------------------------------------------------------
Ran 2 tests in 0.007s

OK
bhagya@bhagya-VirtualBox:~$
```

We use a unit testing tool that supports test discovery. This basically just means it looks at the available files and decides for itself which ones seems like a test file; then it loads the test from those files and runs them.

Unittest's discovery tool

The `unittest` package has a basic but useful built-in test discovery tool. When we run `python -m unittest discover`, it searches the current directory for Python S, whose names start with the word `test`. In addition, it recursively performs the same scan on any subdirectories that contain an `init.py` file. Once it collects the names of all the matching modules, it runs the test just as if we'd specified the modules on the command line ourselves. This can be illustrated using the following code example:

```
bhagya@bhagya-VirtualBox:~$ python3 -m unittest discover -v
test_addition (suite.test_one.BasicTest) ... ok
test_append (suite.test_two.SharedEnv) ... ok
test_replace (suite.test_two.SharedEnv) ... ok

----------------------------------------------------------------------
Ran 3 tests in 0.035s

OK
```

Command-line options in unit test discovery

There are a few command-line options we can use to adjust the behavior of unit test discovery. The first, which we saw in the previous code example, is the −v switch. This switch makes test reports somewhat more verbose. We used it in the previous code so we could see that the discovery had worked properly.

We can also use the −p command-line option (as shown in the following code example) to change the pattern that is used to recognize test files:

```
bhagya@bhagya-VirtualBox:~$ python3 -m unittest discover -v -p '*one.py'
test_addition (suite.test_one.BasicTest) ... ok

----------------------------------------------------------------------
Ran 1 test in 0.000s

OK
bhagya@bhagya-VirtualBox:~$
```

Here, we've changed it so that the filenames ending in the word one.py are recognized as test files.

The unittest discover code also recognizes −s to specify the directory where the test search should start. This is shown in the following code example:

```
bhagya@bhagya-VirtualBox:~$ python3 -m unittest discover -v -s suite/
test_addition (test_one.BasicTest) ... ok
test_append (test_two.SharedEnv) ... ok
test_replace (test_two.SharedEnv) ... ok

----------------------------------------------------------------------
Ran 3 tests in 0.004s

OK
bhagya@bhagya-VirtualBox:~$
```

Notice that by making a suite act as the starting directory for the search, we've stopped it from being recognized as a package containing the test. If that's a problem, we could supplement the −s option with −t (refer to the following code example), which tells you to test where to find the top-level directory for this run:

```
bhagya@bhagya-VirtualBox:~$ python3 -m unittest discover -v -s suite/ -t .
test_addition (suite.test_one.BasicTest) ... ok
test_append (suite.test_two.SharedEnv) ... ok
test_replace (suite.test_two.SharedEnv) ... ok

----------------------------------------------------------------------
Ran 3 tests in 0.004s

OK
bhagya@bhagya-VirtualBox:~$
```

Using both −s and −t, we're able to narrow the test search to a particular subdirectory while still running the tests in the context of a parent directory.

There's a bit of a pitfall to be aware of when using unit test discovery code or any other test discovery that works by importing modules to check whether they contain tests. This pitfall is that the modules are imported.

Most of the time, that's not a problem, but if a piece of test discovery code imports the module that was meant to be a program's entry point, it might result in actually running the program, which is not the desired behavior. It's easy to avoid this problem when we're writing an entry point by wrapping the entry point code in the if '__name__' = = '__main__' statement.

However, if we, or somebody else, skips this check and unittest thinks the file looks like a test file, running unit test discovery code will have surprising results. That's all there is in regard to unittest's test discovery tool. It doesn't have many features, but it does have the features that everybody needs, and there's a good chance that it's all we'll need for the majority of our projects.

For cases where we need more from our test discovery tool, we can use nose, which we'll look at in the next section.

Using nose for unified test discovery and reporting

Note that `nose` is a third-party tool available via `pip` and Python Package Index. It does basically the same job as a unittest `discover` command, but it supports more control and customization as well as recognizing a wider range of tests. It can be installed using the following command line:

```
python3 -m pip install nose
```

```
devesh@devesh-VirtualBox:~$ python3 -m pip install nose
Collecting nose
  Downloading nose-1.3.7-py3-none-any.whl (154kB)
    100% |                                | 163kB 224kB/s
Installing collected packages: nose
Successfully installed nose-1.3.7
You are using pip version 8.1.1, however version 9.0.1 is available.
You should consider upgrading via the 'pip install --upgrade pip' command.
devesh@devesh-VirtualBox:~$
```

Running our tests with nose

We're going to look at two specific features among the many that nose provides. These are:

- It can generate a code coverage report that tells us how much of the code our test actually tested
- It can run tests across multiple processes, allowing them to be executed in parallel on multiple CPUs

In order to get a coverage report, we first need to make sure that the coverage module is installed. We could do this with a simple `pip` command, as follows:

```
python3 -m pip install coverage
```

```
devesh@devesh-VirtualBox:~$ python3 -m pip install coverage
Collecting coverage
  Downloading coverage-4.4.1-cp35-cp35m-manylinux1_x86_64.whl (196kB)
    100% |                                | 204kB 64kB/s
Installing collected packages: coverage
Successfully installed coverage-4.4.1
You are using pip version 8.1.1, however version 9.0.1 is available.
You should consider upgrading via the 'pip install --upgrade pip' command.
devesh@devesh-VirtualBox:~$
```

Once we have the `coverage` module in place, we can enable a coverage report for our test with nothing more than a couple of nose's command-line options.

Strictly speaking, only the `--with-coverage` option is required to enable the coverage report, as shown in the following code example:

```
(nose) $ python3 -m nose --with-coverage --cover-erase
...
Name            Stmts   Miss  Cover
------------------------------------
suite.py            0      0   100%
uncovered.py        8      3    62%
------------------------------------
TOTAL               8      3    62%
------------------------------------------------------------------------
Ran 3 tests in 0.021s

OK
(nose) $ 
```

However, if we don't include `--cover-erase` as well, coverage data from previous test runs will get mixed with our current run, which will make the results harder to interpret.

The cover-package option

There's a third coverage-related command-line option that is sometimes useful. It is the `cover-package` option; it narrows down the code coverage report to only a specific package, as shown in the following code example:

```
(nose) $ python3 -m nose --with-coverage --cover-erase --cover-package=suite
...
Name          Stmts   Miss  Cover
----------------------------------
suite.py          0      0   100%
-------------------------------------------------------------------
Ran 3 tests in 0.019s

OK
(nose) $ 
```

Focusing the report this way can make it easier to read and extract useful information.

Testing multiple worker processes

The other nose feature we're going to look at is the ability to farm out tests to multiple worker processes and thus spread them across the available CPU cores. To test multiple worker processes, we just have to provide the `--processes=` command-line option and tell it how many processes to use. If we pass `-1` to indicate the number of processes, it uses the detected number of CPU cores, which is probably what we want anyway (refer to the following code example):

```
(nose) $ python3 -m nose --processes=-1
. . .
- - - - - - - - - - - - - - - - - - - - - - - - - - - - - - - - - - - - - - - - - - -
Ran 3 tests in 0.092s

OK
(nose) $
```

So, unless we have a specific reason to do otherwise, we should always just use `-1`.

If we look carefully at the preceding code example, we can see that it actually took longer to run our test suite on multiple processes. That's because conducting the tests themselves involves low effort, but it's not the same when it comes to launching a worker process. Fortunately, that's a fixed cost, so when we start running larger test suites that contain more expensive tests, we start seeing the benefits of parallel execution.

This was just a taste of the sort of features that nose supports and that's without writing our own nose plugins to customize it further. It's a very capable system, so if we find ourselves needing a particular feature from our test runner, a good first step is to see whether nose already has that feature.

Summary

In this chapter, we learned how to use the `unittest` and `unittest.mock` packages to write an automated test; we also learned the process of test-driven development. Next, we saw how to use `unittest.mock` to control the environment that our test code runs in so that the test can remain focused on making sure one thing works properly. Post this, we learned how to run a test using Python's built-in unit test tools, and finally, we discussed how to take advantage of a couple of features of the nose test runner.

In the next chapter, we're going to take a look at the reactive programming paradigm and RxPY.

10
Reactive Programming

In the previous chapter, you learned about unit testing and the `unittest.mock` package. In this chapter, you will get a handle on the concepts of reactive programming and then take a look at the RxPY reactive programming framework. We'll work on solidifying your conceptual understanding of reactive programming and put together a very bare-bones reactive programming system from scratch.

In this chapter, we will cover the following topics:

- What does reactive programming mean?
- Building a simple reactive programming framework
- Using the **Reactive Extensions for Python (RxPY)**

The concept of reactive programming

There are a lot of different and valid ways that I could define reactive programming. It's a matter of perspective and focus. Which of them is the best definition? We're going to cover several in this section.

Perhaps, the most fundamental definition of reactive programming, at least in terms of what we need to think about to implement a reactive programming system, is that it's a publish/subscribe model of event handling. The following diagram illustrates the basic reactive event handling:

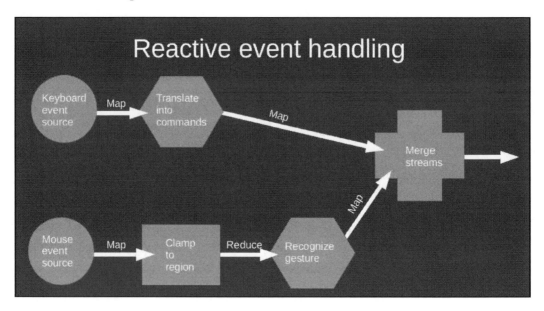

In the traditional nomenclature of reactive programming, there are **observables** and **observers,** which encapsulate the behavior of event publishers and event subscribers, respectively. In a reactive programming system, everything, or at least as much as possible, is an observable or an observer. So far, so good, but the publish/subscribe model by itself isn't really that exciting.

Reactive programming comes into its own when we recognize that an observable is conceptually very similar to a list, which means functional programming tools, such as map and reduce, have powerful analogues that apply to observables. So, the second definition of reactive programming is that it's **event-driven functional** programming.

The idea that we could, for example, take two observables, map a function over one of them, merge the result with the other, and reduce that merge sequence to a new value is a powerful one. We could describe all of the operations we want to perform ahead of time and whenever a new value comes out of one of the root observables, it will cascade through our whole processing chain, without further effort on our part.

Functional programming operations are mostly stateless and when they're not, the state is at least easy to define and keep contained. This means that our event-driven, mostly-stateless reactive programming systems are very well-suited to asynchronous or parallel execution. Thus, our third definition of reactive programming is that it's a systematic way of writing high-performance asynchronous or parallel code.

So, what is reactive programming? Let's bundle those definitions together. Reactive programming is an event-driven paradigm in which event sources can have functional operators applied to them to create new event sources. This is desirable because it results in programs that work well in asynchronous or parallel execution environments.

Building a simple reactive programming framework

You have gained an understanding of what reactive programming means in a theoretical way. Now, we're going to get very concrete and build a simple reactive programming system, then build a demo so we can watch it in action. The roots of formalized reactive programming are in statically typed languages, particularly C#. That's of little concern to us as users of a language based around dynamic typing, but it does mean that the standard presentation of these ideas is heavily intertwined with types, templates, interfaces, and anonymous functions. We'll be a little less Pythonic here and perhaps a little more C#-ish. That said, let's move on to the coding.

Observers

Arguably, the single most fundamental element of a reactive programming system is the observer interface. The definition of how we can notify an object that the next item in a sequence is watching it is available. What we're starting with in the following code example is an abstract base class, the closest Python equivalent to a C# interface:

```
class Observer(abc.ABC):
    @abc.abstractmethod
    def on_event(self, event):
        pass

    def on_exception(self, exception):
        pass

    def on_complete(self):
        pass
```

Our `Observer` class doesn't define any functionality at all, just method names and signatures, and guarantees that classes which inherit from it will have to implement at least the `on_event` method. For a complete functionality, they'd have to implement `on_exception` and `on_complete` as well, but that's not required.

So, the intent is that an `Observer` class will have its `on_event` method called once for each element of the sequence, followed by its `on_complete` method if the sequence terminates while the observer is watching it. If something goes sideways, the `on_exception` method would be called instead.

For an `Observer` class to be useful, there must also be an `Observable` class. So, let's see the beginning of that class.

Observables

Like `Observer`, `Observable` is an abstract base class, although in this case, we provide meaningful default implementations of all of its functionality.

The `subscribe` method, shown in the following code example, is how an `Observer` class connects to the `Observable` class, registering itself as a consumer of the events that the `Observable` class emits:

```
class Observable(abc.ABC):
    def __init__(self):
        self.observers = set()
        self.complete = False

    def subscribe(self, subscriber):
        if not isinstance(subscriber, Observer):
            raise ValueError('Only Observer objects are valid subscribers')
        self.observers.add(subscriber)
```

Emitting events

There are three methods which take care of emitting events. These are as follows:

- One for sending normal events
- One for sending exceptions
- One for sending a "this sequence has ended" event

These are shown in the following code example:

```
class Observable(abc.ABC):
    def __init__(self):
        self.observers = set()
        self.complete = False

    def subscribe(self, subscriber):
        if not isinstance(subscriber, Observer):
            raise ValueError('Only Observer objects are valid subscribers')
        self.observers.add(subscriber)

    def _event(self, event):
        if self.complete:
            raise RuntimeError("Can't send events on a completed Observable")
        for obs in self.observers:
            obs.on_event(event)

    def _exception(self, exception):
        if self.complete:
            raise RuntimeError("Can't send exceptions on a completed Observable")
        for obs in self.observers:
            obs.on_exception(event)

    def _complete(self):
        if self.complete:
            raise RuntimeError("Can't complete an already completed Observable")
        self.complete = True
        for obs in self.observers:
            obs.on_complete()
```

In each case, they do a bit of error checking, then loop through the registered observers and invoke the appropriate method. These methods have names prefixed with a single underscore (_), marking them as not part of the public interface of the `Observable` class. They are helpers to make subclasses easier to write.

That can't possibly be a complete reactive programming system, can it? Yes and no. It is fundamentally complete, but it's lacking a great many refinements and in no way is it ready for a production environment. It will serve nicely as the spine for our demo program though, so let's move on to that.

Building the observable sequence

For our demo, we'll make a program that prints messages loosely representing the sounds we might hear in a zoo. The animals will be represented as observables emitting events, representing sounds at random intervals. We'll use merging and mapping to combine and modify the event sequences, before finally printing out the resulting sequence.

So, first of all, we have our `Animal` class, which is an observable, and the `AnimalEvent` helper class. The `Animal` class contains some basic information and a coroutine, which will run asynchronously and occasionally send events to the observers of the `Animal` class as shown in the following code example:

```python
class AnimalEvent:
    def __init__(self, source, action, value = ''):
        self.source = source
        self.action = action
        self.value = value


class Animal(Observable):
    def __init__(self, name, sound):
        super().__init__()
        self.name = name
        self.sound = sound

    async def run(self):
        while True:
            await asyncio.sleep(random.random() * 10)

            if random.random() < 0.01:
                self._event(AnimalEvent(self, 'die'))
                self._complete()
                return

            self._event(AnimalEvent(self, 'noise', self.sound))
```

Looking at the preceding code, we can see that an animal is effectively a sequence of noise events, then a die event, immediately followed by the completion of the sequence.

We want some of our animals to be capable of creating loud noises. Instead of adding that capability to the Animal class, we'll create a mapping over the sequence of events, which replaces randomly selected noise events with loud noise events.

This mapping is both an observer, so that it can subscribe to the sequence of events, and an observable because the sequence of modified events is still a sequence of events and not much use if another observable can't subscribe to it.

This is fundamentally what happens in any reactive programming system when we apply an operator to an observable sequence to create a new observable sequence. However, in almost every case, a real reactive system provides us with a quicker, easier, and usually more efficient way of doing it.

 Actually creating a class that's both observer and observable is rare indeed!

Illustrating a stream of animal events

There's one more piece we need before we start putting things together and that's a way to display a stream of animal events. Another observer is the obvious choice for that and it turns out to be quite easy, as you can see in the following code example:

```python
class Output(Observer):
    def __init__(self, *sources):
        super().__init__()
        for source in sources:
            source.subscribe(self)

    def on_event(self, event):
        if event.action == 'die':
            print(event.source.name, 'died!')
        else:
            print(event.source.name, event.value)
```

The code for a new observer is similar to what we've already seen; all we need is a constructor and an appropriate on_event method.

Composing an observable sequence

Now that we've got all the pieces, how do we put them together to achieve our goal? Well, first we make our animal objects and then use the `SometimesLoud` and `Output` classes to create our modified composite sequence and display it as shown in the following code example from `animals.py`:

```python
def zoo():
    elephant = Animal('Lucretia', 'trumpets')
    lion = Animal('Arnold', 'roars')
    fox = Animal('Betty', 'goes chacha-chacha-chacha-chow')
    snake = Animal('Jake', 'hisses')

    out = Output(fox, snake, SometimesLoud(elephant, lion))

    return asyncio.gather(elephant.run(), lion.run(), fox.run(), snake.run())
```

Then, we need to schedule the run methods of each animal for asynchronous execution via `asyncio`, which happens implicitly in this example when we pass them as parameters together in our __main__.py file:

```python
def zoo():
    elephant = Animal('Lucretia', 'trumpets')
    lion = Animal('Arnold', 'roars')
    fox = Animal('Betty', 'goes chacha-chacha-chacha-chow')
    snake = Animal('Jake', 'hisses')

    out = Output(fox, snake, SometimesLoud(elephant, lion))

    return asyncio.gather(elephant.run(), lion.run(), fox.run(),
snake.run())
```

```python
import asyncio

from .animals import zoo


if __name__ == '__main__':
    asyncio.get_event_loop().run_until_complete(zoo())
```

Our __main__.py file actually runs the `asyncio` event loop. So, now we can just sit back and watch the pseudo cacophony of our imaginary zoo, as shown in the following output window:

```
$ python3 -m zoo
Jake hisses
Arnold roars loudly
Lucretia trumpets loudly
Arnold roars
Betty goes chacha-chacha-chacha-chow
Betty goes chacha-chacha-chacha-chow
Arnold roars
Jake hisses
Arnold roars
Lucretia trumpets
Betty goes chacha-chacha-chacha-chow
Jake hisses
```

Did you notice how the meat of our program is boiled down to a single line of code?

Sure, we have a whole file devoted to the framework, but that's reusable. We also have the `SometimesLoud` and `Output` classes, but the only reason they're here is so we can see exactly what happens at each step of this program.

In a real system, `Output` and `SometimesLoud` would have used built-in functionality that mapped the function on the sequence, as we'll see in the next section. All of this leaves us with a single line of code that composites several observable sequences and transformations, and defines most of the behavior of the program. This one line demonstrates the power of reactive programming.

Using the reactive extensions for Python (RxPY)

Now that we have a basic understanding of reactive programming under our belts, let's look at one of the more widely used reactive programming frameworks called **Reactive Extensions**, which is often shortened to **ReactiveX**, or simply **Rx**.

Rx is not part of a standard Python installation, so we'll need to use `pip` to install it. No problem; it's only a single command, if you prefer to install to your Python system library instead of user library, or you are working in a virtual created by the `--user` from this command, as shown here:

```
(rx) $ pip install rx
Collecting rx
  Downloading Rx-1.5.2-py2.py3-none-any.whl (183kB)
    100% |                              | 184kB 2.1MB/s
Installing collected packages: rx
Successfully installed rx-1.5.2
You are using pip version 8.1.1, however version 8.1.2 is available.
You should consider upgrading via the 'pip install --upgrade pip' command.
(rx) $
```

Once we have Rx installed, we can move on to the fun stuff.

Translating our zoo demo into Rx

Like our example in the previous section, Rx provides `Observer` and `Observable` classes, and they encompass the same basic functionality.

The largest visible difference is that the `Observable` class of Rx has a large number of factory methods that could be used to construct special-purpose observables, especially, observables that produce a sequence based on one or more other observable sequences. In other words, most of the operators and operations that we'll use to construct a reactive dataflow are methods of the `Observable` class.

Let's take a moment to rewrite our demo from the previous section in Rx and we'll see what that means in practice.

The `AnimalEvent` class can stay the same, since it's just a data structure and doesn't know anything about who's using it for what. Our `Animal` class changes quite a bit. The run coroutine method goes away and in its place we have a somewhat simpler `generate_event` method (refer to the following code example):

```python
class Animal:
    def __init__(self, name, sound):
        self.name = name
        self.sound = sound
        self.alive = True

    def generate_event(self):
        if random.random() < 0.01:
            self.alive = False
            return AnimalEvent(self, 'die')
        return AnimalEvent(self, 'noise', self.sound)

    def as_observable(self, scheduler):
        return rx.Observable.generate_with_relative_time(
            self,                                # initial state
            (lambda x: self.alive),              # continue condition
            (lambda x: self),                    # next state
            (lambda x: self.generate_event()),   # get next value
            (lambda x: random.random() * 10),    # how long before next cycle
            scheduler
        )
```

 That name isn't significant by the way; it's just a reasonable name I picked because it describes what the method does.

As shown in the preceding code, the `generate_event` method by itself doesn't encompass the entire functionality of the old run coroutine method, though. It knows how to emit an event, but it doesn't know how to wait a short while and do it again. That's where the `as_observable` method comes into play.

Observable factory methods

The `as_observable` method uses one of the factory methods of the `Observable` class to create an observable sequence. This sequence is backed up by what is functionally a generator, although it's not implemented as one because that concept doesn't exist in every language that Rx is portable to.

So, instead of a real generator, we're providing it with a state variable, which in this case is just the animal instance, along with functions it could call to check whether the sequences continue, update the state, get the next value in the sequence, or determine how long to wait before producing the next value. The factory method also accepts a scheduler object, which we'll discuss later in this section. So, what we're asking for in this code is an observable that produces animal events at random intervals from 0 to 10 seconds. Now, the `Animal` class may be a little simpler than it used to be; there's not a big difference.

However, let's take a look at what happens with the `SometimesLoud` and `Output` classes (refer to the following code example); they're not classes anymore, just functions, and are significantly simpler:

```
def sometimes_loud(event):
    if event.action == 'noise' and random.random() < 0.25:
        return AnimalEvent(event.source,
                           event.action,
                           '{} loudly'.format(event.value))
    return event


def output(event):
    if event.action == 'die':
        print(event.source.name, 'died!')
    else:
        print(event.source.name, event.value)
```

The `sometimes_loud` function takes an event and returns an event, and we'll use it to map from one observable sequence of events into a new one, just as you'd expect in a functional programming environment. The `output` function takes an event and returns none, which is again what we'd expect for a `side_effect` in a functional system.

Explaining the observable sequence of events

So, now that we have our observable factory method and function to take and return an event; what do we need to do to put it all together? First, we will create an `asyncio` scheduler. Next comes the interesting part, where we will tell the computer how to combine and process those observable sequences.

Creating an asyncio scheduler

We can create an `asyncio` scheduler using a simple command, as shown here:

```
scheduler = rx.concurrency.AsyncIOScheduler ()
```

This is an Rx scheduler that specifically integrates with an `asyncio` event loop. Rx contains quite a few different scheduler implementations that integrate with various event loops available in Python, as well as one that uses Python threads to implement scheduling.

Regardless of which scheduler we use, the scheduler's job will be to decide when time-based elements of our event pipeline occur. This means that in this example, the scheduler is going to be deciding when our animal observables produce new values.

After creating the scheduler, we create the animal objects and their observable sequence of events. The animal objects are the easy part, as shown here:

```
elephant = Animal('Lucretia', 'trumpets').as_observable(scheduler)
lion = Animal('Arnold', 'roars').as_observable(scheduler)
fox = Animal('Betty', 'goes chacha-chacha-chacha-chow').as_observable(scheduler)
snake = Animal('Jake', 'hisses').as_observable(scheduler)
```

Combining and processing observable sequences

For combining and processing the observable sequences, we have three steps to follow. These are explained here:

- First, we merge the elephant and lion sequences into a single combined sequence, and process that sequence through our `sometimes_loud` function to create a new sequence we call `louder`, as shown in the following code example:

  ```
  louder = rx.Observable.merge(elephant,
  lion).select(sometimes_loud)
  ```

  The `select` method used in that line is the direct equivalent of the map function in a functional programming environment.

- Next, we merge the `louder` sequence with the remaining animal sequences and tell the system that whenever a new value arrives at the front of that merge sequence, it should call the output function on that value:

```
out = rx.Observable.merge(fox, snake, louder)
.do_action(on_next = output)
```

The `do_action` method used in this example is not equivalent to map because it doesn't transform the sequence; it just performs an action on each element of it.

The `do_action` method is for side_effects.

- Finally, as shown as follows, we subscribe to the `on_completed` event on the out observable sequence, which is the same as the sequence merging all event streams into one, since the `do_action` operation returns its input sequence unchanged:

```
done = asyncio.Future()
out.subscribe(on_completed = (lambda:
done.set_result(True)))
return done
```

When the sequence is complete, we set a result value on the `done` future. Since we used that feature as the perimeter to run until complete in our `main.py` file, setting its result value terminates the `asyncio` event loop and our program ends.

The complete code listing for the `animals.py` file in this section is as follows:

```
def zoo():
    scheduler = rx.concurrency.AsyncIOScheduler()

    elephant = Animal('Lucretia', 'trumpets').as_observable(scheduler)
    lion = Animal('Arnold', 'roars').as_observable(scheduler)
    fox = Animal('Betty', 'goes chacha-chacha-chacha-chow').as_observable(scheduler)
    snake = Animal('Jake', 'hisses').as_observable(scheduler)

    louder = rx.Observable.merge(elephant, lion).select(sometimes_loud)

    out = rx.Observable.merge(fox, snake, louder).do_action(on_next = output)

    done = asyncio.Future()

    out.subscribe(on_completed = (lambda: done.set_result(True)))

    return done
```

Miscellaneous observable factory methods

The demo that we just worked through has shown us the `merge`, `merge.select`, and `generate_with_relative_time` factory methods of `Observable`, but that's just the tip of the iceberg.

There are so many observable factories (a sample of which is shown in the following image) that it would take more time than we have, just to get a short description of each one:

```
rx.Observable.group_join(                rx.Observable.window_with_time_or_count(
rx.Observable.if_then(                   rx.Observable.with_latest_from(
rx.Observable.ignore_elements(           rx.Observable.zip(
rx.Observable.interval(                  rx.Observable.zip_array(
rx.Observable.is_empty(                  rx.Observable.zip_list(
>>> rx.Observable.
```

Each of them gives us a useful way of constructing an observable, usually, but not always, based on one or more other observables.

Python's interactive shell and `help` function are our friends here. There's a lot to be learned by poking around in the `Observable` class. In the meantime, we're going to talk about a few of the very best observable factory methods that we haven't seen yet.

The Observable.create method

First on that list is `Observable.create` shown in the following code example. This is the recommended way of creating a completely customized observable:

```
rx.Observable.create((lambda obs: obs.on_next('Hi!')))
```

The `create` method has callable as its parameter and calls that callable each time an observer subscribes to the observable.

In the preceding code example, we created an observable that says `Hi!` when an observer subscribes and then never produces another value; not the most useful of sequences, but it serves to illustrate the idea.

We can take the basic framework and construct an observable with any behavior we like from it, without subclassing the observable class and without re-implementing, probably incorrectly, the internal machinery that keeps observables synchronized and functioning properly in an asynchronous or parallel environment.

The Observable.select_many method

Next is `Observable.select_many`. This time, let's take a look at what Python's `help` function can show us, using following command:

```
help(rx.Observable.select_many)
```

This should give you the following description:

```
Help on function select_many in module rx.linq.observable.selectmany:

select_many(self, selector, result_selector=None)
    One of the Following:
    Projects each element of an observable sequence to an observable
    sequence and merges the resulting observable sequences into one
    observable sequence.

    1 - source.select_many(lambda x: Observable.range(0, x))

    Or:
    Projects each element of an observable sequence to an observable
    sequence, invokes the result selector for the source element and each
    of the corresponding inner sequence's elements, and merges the results
    into one observable sequence.

    1 - source.select_many(lambda x: Observable.range(0, x), lambda x, y: x + y)

    Or:
    Projects each element of the source observable sequence to the other
    observable sequence and merges the resulting observable sequences into
    one observable sequence.

    1 - source.select_many(Observable.from_([1,2,3]))

    Keyword arguments:
    selector -- A transform function to apply to each element or an
        observable sequence to project each element from the source
        sequence onto.
    result_selector -- [Optional] A transform function to apply to each
        element of the intermediate sequence.
```

This observable factory method is a more generalized version of select. Here, select applies a function to each member of the sequence to create a new sequence from the function return values, and `select_many` expects a function that returns an observable sequence and concatenates those sequences.

This means that the function applied by `select_many` can remove elements from the sequence by returning an empty sequence and it can insert values by returning a sequence containing more than one element.

As with select, the values added to the result aren't necessarily the same values that were passed to the function either, so `select_many` can produce a sequence containing more or fewer values than the input sequence and the values can be determined however we choose.

Empty, return_value, and from_iterable factory methods

Empty sequences and sequences of one value are easy to create using the `empty` and `return_value` factory methods, respectively. These can be shown using two commands, which are illustrated with their help pages respectively.

```
help (rx.Observable.empty)
```

This command will lead us to the following help page:

```
Help on method empty in module rx.linq.observable.empty:

empty(scheduler=None) method of builtins.type instance
    Returns an empty observable sequence, using the specified scheduler
    to send out the single OnCompleted message.

    1 - res = rx.Observable.empty()
    2 - res = rx.Observable.empty(rx.Scheduler.timeout)

    scheduler -- Scheduler to send the termination call on.

    Returns an observable sequence with no elements.
```

Similarly, in the case of `return_value`, we can use this command:

```
help (rx.Observable.return_value)
```

We'll get this help page explaining how to use the method:

```
Help on method return_value in module rx.linq.observable.returnvalue:

return_value(value, scheduler=None) method of builtins.type instance
    Returns an observable sequence that contains a single element,
    using the specified scheduler to send out observer messages.
    There is an alias called 'just'.

    example
    res = rx.Observable.return(42)
    res = rx.Observable.return(42, rx.Scheduler.timeout)

    Keyword arguments:
    value -- Single element in the resulting observable sequence.
    scheduler -- [Optional] Scheduler to send the single element on. If
        not specified, defaults to Scheduler.immediate.

    Returns an observable sequence containing the single specified
    element.
```

Similarly, it's easy to construct an observable sequence of any already known series of objects using the `of` or `from_iterable` factory methods.

The where factory method

While we could use `select_many` to remove unwanted events from an observable sequence, it's easier to use the `where` method. Let's look at the help information for the `where` method:

```
help (rx.Observable.where)
```

This method applies a callable to each element of the input observable sequence and returns an observable sequence containing only those elements for which the callable returned true. The following image shows the help description:

```
Help on function where in module rx.linq.observable.where:

where(self, predicate)
    Filters the elements of an observable sequence based on a predicate
    by incorporating the element's index.

    1 - source.filter(lambda value: value < 10)
    2 - source.filter(lambda value, index: value < 10 or index < 10)

    Keyword arguments:
    :param Observable self: Observable sequence to filter.
    :param (T, <int>) -> bool predicate: A function to test each source element
        for a condition; the
        second parameter of the function represents the index of the source
        element.

    :returns: An observable sequence that contains elements from the input
    sequence that satisfy the condition.
    :rtype: Observable
```

Now we saw that there are fundamental ways to add and remove observable sequences, so what about processing them? We could just use `select` and `select_many` to do all of our processing, but Rx provides us with many more methods, such as `min`, `max`, `average`, `distinct`, `slice`, and `zip`, just to name a few of the tools available to us. I highly recommend that you investigate the Rx framework in more detail.

Summary

In this chapter, we discussed what reactive programming is and implemented a bare-bones reactive framework, and used it to implement a demo program to help us get a handle on the concepts. We looked at the Reactive Extensions for Python, and used them to re-implement our zoo demo. We finished by looking at some of the broader possibilities of the Rx framework.

In the next chapter, we'll look at microservices, which are very small server processes that are meant to work together to create the desired results.

11
Microservices

In the previous chapter, we looked at reactive programming and the ReactiveX framework. In this chapter, we're going to take a look at what a microservice is, why we might want to structure our programs as microservices, and how to use some common Python tools to create them. You'll learn how to use the Flask package to quickly and easily construct a microservice that uses HTTP and **representational state transfer, (REST)**, to provide its interface. We're also going to look at using the nameko package to create microservices that communicate using remote procedure calls instead of HTTP methods.

In this chapter, we will cover the following topics:

- Microservices and the advantages of process isolation
- Building high-level microservices with Flask
- Building high-level microservices with nameko

Microservices and the advantages of process isolation

In this section, we'll look at microservices from a conceptual perspective. When we need a new feature for a project, there's a temptation to just add it to the project's main program and continue on from there. Sometimes, that's entirely appropriate, but in many cases, it's actually better to make the feature a distinct program in its own right.

Advantages of the microservice architecture

There are several reasons why a feature might be better off when less tightly integrated into the system. The most important ones are **flexibility**, **scalability**, and **durability**.

Understanding the flexibility benefit is easy. Modular programs inherently consist of a bunch of modules that we can reuse in the future. So, every time we write our code as an independent module with a well-defined interface, we're making an investment that will make it easier to adapt to the changes that come in the future.

The scalability advantage comes into play when our modules are actually separate processes, allowing separate instances to be run on multiple processors, with the load balanced across them.

The durability advantage also comes into play when the modules are processes because processes are mostly safe from the bugs that crop up in other processes, also because a failed process can often be restarted without needing to take down the whole system.

Applying the microservice architecture to web servers

Flexibility, scalability and durability are the same advantages that drove the development of microkernel operating systems back in the 1980s, but the term microservice (refer to following image) specifically refers to applying them to web applications:

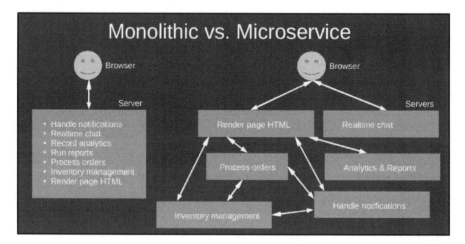

This means that instead of writing one server program that handles all the logic of our web application, we'll write one or more servers that handle most of the frontend work and call on a bunch of different special-purpose servers to handle all the backend work and any remaining parts of the frontend.

Each special-purpose server should do a single well-defined job as well as possible and not care about anything. Those special-purpose servers are microservices, and using a microservice design gives us better uptime. Uptime lets us scale up to take advantage of a server farm or a cloud hosting system and helps us adapt to the ever-changing web more quickly.

So, to recap, when our server is actually a collection of servers, each of which has a narrow and well-defined job to do, and does only that, we're using a microservice architecture. As an added benefit, the interfaces between our microservices constitute an application programming interface. So, if we get to a place where we want to expose an API for the world to use, all we have to do is adjust our authentication and authorization code, and possibly our routers, to allow external entities to access some of those interfaces.

Building high-level microservices with Flask

So, we had a look at what a microservice is and why structuring our servers as collection of microservices is helpful. Now, let's take a look at the practicalities and use Flask to construct a functioning microservice.

Microservices can be pretty easily divided into those that use web technologies, such as HTTP, to communicate with each other and those that use a dedicated inter-process communication or a remote-procedure-called mechanism to communicate.

There are advantages to each, depending on the specific needs of a project and neither is inherently easier to work with. However, I'm going to refer to microservices that use web technologies to communicate as *high level* because they are inherently closer to the level at which users operate. Conversely, I'll refer to microservices that use specialized protocols as *low level*. In this section, we'll look at high-level microservices, which usually use HTTP to communicate and provide REST-based programming interfaces.

Using stateless protocols for communication makes these microservices easy to load balance and easy to swap in and out for maintenance. For this type of microservice, we can use any of Python's several production quality web application frameworks or toolkits, but we're going to use Flask.

Installing Flask

Flask is laser-focused on making it easy to write handlers for HTTP requests and doesn't really do anything else. That makes it very well-suited for writing a microservice that processes a few specific requests while using minimal resources.

Flask isn't part of a Python standard library, but it's easily installed using `pip`, as shown in the following command line:

```
$python3 -m pip install flask
```

As always, you can add `--user` to the command to install Flask into your personal Python package library, or you can install it into a virtual environment if you prefer.

Creating endpoints for a RESTful API in Flask

Flask is designed to interface with a frontend web server or proxy using the **Web Server Gateway Interface** (**WSGI**), which is standard for Python web applications. However, we'll just use its built-in development server for our simple little demonstration. So, what shall we build?

Building a microservice to maintain a database

Let's build a microservice that maintains a database of information about people-first name, last name, age, and for interest's sake, whether or not they are members of a particular club.

We'll use the `POST`, `GET`, `PUT`, and `DELETE` methods of HTTP to allow the clients of the microservice to create, access, update, and remove records from the database. Also, we'll provide the data in JSON format, but accept the input using the normal HTTP form encoding.

These choices are all very normal. The only, slightly-less-common choice would be to have incoming data in JSON format as well, which we accommodate by calling the `request.get_json` function of Flask when we need the data.

So, which boilerplate code do we need to get a Flask microservice on its feet? Not much, as it turns out. The following two command lines are sufficient to get the Flask system in place:

```
import flask
app = flask.Flask('Demo Flask')
```

These lines don't actually do anything except return *404 Not Found* errors in response to any request, but they'll respond. So, how do we make Flask handle a request? Let's take a look.

Making Flask handle a request

There are actually two ways to make Flask handle a request: one way is incredibly simple and the other is more flexible and better encapsulated.

The simpler way is to use the `@app.route` decorator to tell Flask that a particular function will handle requests for a given path, as shown in the following code example:

```
@app.route('/example')
def example():
    return "This is an example"
```

That's all that's needed, apart from making the function actually do something useful.

However, for our microservice, we want to use HTTP methods on the same path to produce different results. We can use an `app.route` decorator and a bunch of `if` and `else if` blocks in the function to handle that, but there's a better way, which is explained using the following code example and that you can find in the `endpoint.py` file in the download pack:

```python
import flask.views

class Endpoint(flask.views.MethodView):
    def post(self):
        flask.abort(405)

    def get(self, id):
        flask.abort(405)

    def put(self, id):
        flask.abort(405)

    def delete(self, id):
        flask.abort(405)

    @classmethod
    def register(class_, app, base = '', default_id = None):
        view = class_.as_view(class_.__name__)

        # When no ID is provided, accept GET and use the default ID
        app.add_url_rule('{}/{}'.format(base, class_.__name__.lower()),
                        defaults = {'id': default_id},
                        view_func = view,
                        methods = ['GET'])

        # When no ID is provided, accept POST
        app.add_url_rule('{}/{}'.format(base, class_.__name__.lower()),
                        view_func = view,
                        methods = ['POST'])

        # When an ID is provided, accept GET, PUT, and DELETE
        app.add_url_rule('{}/{}/<int:id>'.format(base, class_.__name__.lower()),
                        view_func = view,
                        methods = ['GET', 'PUT', 'DELETE'])
```

Flask supports pluggable view classes and specifically has a `MethodView` class that has a different handler function for each HTTP method, as you can see in the first four function definitions in our class. The appropriate function processes each request based on which HTTP method was used.

There's a slight complication to this because we don't actually always want to use the same path. Sometimes, we want an object `id` in the path and sometimes we don't. This is only a small complication though, because we can register the same pluggable view on several different combinations of path and method, which is exactly what the `endpoint.register` function in `endpoint.py` does, as you can see in the code example.

Each registration of `view` consists of one call to `app.add_url_rule`:

- The first one registers the `GET` method with no object `id` and fills in values to use for the `id` parameter when calling the `GET` function
- The second one registers the `POST` method with no `id` and no default because our `POST` function doesn't accept an `id` parameter at all
- The third one registers the `GET`, `PUT`, and `DELETE` methods when there is an `id` parameter

These registrations cover all the use cases common to a single programming interface endpoint in REST.

Running and connecting to our microservice using Flask

Now that we have our method dispatching ready, how about we put together our actual handlers for manipulating person objects? We can do it using the following code found in the `service.py` file:

```python
import flask
import json

from .endpoint import Endpoint
from .person import Person


class PersonAPI(Endpoint):
    def post(self):
        first_name = flask.request.form['first_name']
        last_name = flask.request.form['last_name']
        age = int(flask.request.form['age'])
        try:
            member = flask.request.form['member'] == 'true'
        except KeyError:
            member = False

        person = Person.create(first_name, last_name, age, member)

        return json.dumps(person.as_dict()), 200, {'Content-Type': 'application/json'}

    def get(self, id):
        if id is None:
            return json.dumps([x.as_dict() for x in Person.list()]), 200, {'Content-Type': 'application/json'}

        try:
            person = Person.load(id)
        except KeyError:
            return json.dumps({'error': 'invalid id'}), 404, {'Content-Type': 'application/json'}

        return json.dumps(person.as_dict()), 200, {'Content-Type': 'application/json'}

    def put(self, id):
        try:
            person = Person.load(id)
        except KeyError:
            return json.dumps({'error': 'invalid id'}), 404, {'Content-Type': 'application/json'}

        def update(field_name, proc = (lambda x: x)):
            try:
                setattr(person, field_name, proc(flask.request.form[field_name]))
            except KeyError:
                pass
            ...
```

For the detailed code, please refer to the code files.

From the preceding code example, we find the following:

- We see our `PersonAPI` class, which has one function for each of the operations we want to enable on our `person` database.
- For the `POST` and `PUT` functions, we get data from the request using the `request.form` object, which is a dictionary-like object containing the decoded data from the request body.

 This looks like it's not thread-safe, but it actually is. Everything in Flask is multithread and multiprocess safe; it's just wrapped in a simplifying semantic layer that simulates a single-threaded single-process system.

- The `POST` function doesn't have any code to handle missing data, except for the member value. This is because if we try to access a missing value from `request.form`, an exception is raised that causes Flask to return a *400 Bad Request* error, which is exactly the right thing to do in this case.
- The `PUT` function, on the other hand, handles those exceptions itself, so that it can decide which values to update and which to leave alone.
- The `GET` function might be called with an integer `id` or with `None` for the `id` parameter and needs to handle both cases. This is easily done with an `if` statement.
- In the case where the `id` parameter is a number, the `GET` function is supposed to return the state of the object with that `id` parameter. If `id` is `None`, it is supposed to return a list of all of the objects.

All the methods return JSON-formatted data, which is done using Python's standard `json` package and specifically the `json.dumps` function, which transforms Python data structures into JSON-formatted strings.

We also need to provide the content type header with the value of application JSON as a matter of good practice. Between these two things in the return statement, we're also providing the HTTP status. This could be omitted, but since we're returning error codes in some places, it makes sense to include the status code even when it's not an error.

Test running the microservice

To do a test run of our microservice, we need to start up Flask (using the following command) and tell it to serve our microservice:

For Unix/Linux and macOS, run the following command:

```
export FLASK_APP=demo_flaskpython3 -m flask run
```

For Windows, run the following command:

```
set FLASK_APP=demo_flaskpython3 -m flask run
```

The `demo_flask` package also contains a module called `test.py` that we can use as a client that connects to our microservice and put it through its paces. It will add, delete, list, and modify a couple of database entries and also try out a bad post request to show that the error handling is working.

There's one more part of the Flask demo microservice that we haven't talked about and won't in detail. That is the `person.py` file, which contains a simple interface with a SQLite3 database for actually storing and retrieving objects. Feel free to look at it, of course, but it's not particularly relevant to the topics of the chapter, and a production system should probably use SQLAlchemy, Redis, CouchDB, and so on.

Building high-level microservices with nameko

In this section, we'll take a look at **nameko**, which will help us put together a microservice that communicates using the **Advanced Message Queuing Protocol** (**AMQP**), which we can safely think of as a **Remote Procedure Call** (**RPC**) protocol, though that's actually only a part of what it does.

Installing nameko

Using HTTP to define the interface for our microservice has the advantages of familiarity and good integration with web technologies, but there's a certain amount of overhead involved in mapping the request and input data onto the functions and parameters that are actually meaningful to us.

We can come up with abstractions that hide that part of the process, of course. That's essentially what the authors of nameko did, although they use AMQP instead of HTTP to transport data and events.

Installing nameko itself is easy. Use pretty much the same `pip` command we always use, as shown here:

```
python3 -m pip install nameko
```

The output of the preceding command is as follows:

```
devesh@devesh-VirtualBox:~$ python3 -m pip install nameko
Collecting nameko
  Using cached nameko-2.6.0-py2.py3-none-any.whl
Collecting mock>=1.2 (from nameko)
  Using cached mock-2.0.0-py2.py3-none-any.whl
Collecting path.py>=6.2 (from nameko)
  Using cached path.py-10.3.1-py2.py3-none-any.whl
Collecting eventlet>=0.16.1 (from nameko)
  Using cached eventlet-0.21.0-py2.py3-none-any.whl
Collecting pyyaml>=3.10 (from nameko)
Collecting wrapt>=1.0.0 (from nameko)
Collecting werkzeug>=0.9 (from nameko)
  Using cached Werkzeug-0.12.2-py2.py3-none-any.whl
Collecting kombu<4,>=3.0.1 (from nameko)
  Using cached kombu-3.0.37-py2.py3-none-any.whl
Collecting six>=1.9.0 (from nameko)
  Using cached six-1.10.0-py2.py3-none-any.whl
Collecting requests>=1.2.0 (from nameko)
  Using cached requests-2.18.1-py2.py3-none-any.whl
Collecting pbr>=0.11 (from mock>=1.2->nameko)
  Using cached pbr-3.1.1-py2.py3-none-any.whl
Collecting greenlet>=0.3 (from eventlet>=0.16.1->nameko)
  Using cached greenlet-0.4.12-cp35-cp35m-manylinux1_x86_64.whl
Collecting enum-compat (from eventlet>=0.16.1->nameko)
Collecting amqp<2.0,>=1.4.9 (from kombu<4,>=3.0.1->nameko)
  Using cached amqp-1.4.9-py2.py3-none-any.whl
Collecting anyjson>=0.3.3 (from kombu<4,>=3.0.1->nameko)
Collecting urllib3<1.22,>=1.21.1 (from requests>=1.2.0->nameko)
  Using cached urllib3-1.21.1-py2.py3-none-any.whl
Collecting idna<2.6,>=2.5 (from requests>=1.2.0->nameko)
  Using cached idna-2.5-py2.py3-none-any.whl
Collecting chardet<3.1.0,>=3.0.2 (from requests>=1.2.0->nameko)
  Using cached chardet-3.0.4-py2.py3-none-any.whl
Collecting certifi>=2017.4.17 (from requests>=1.2.0->nameko)
  Using cached certifi-2017.4.17-py2.py3-none-any.whl
Installing collected packages: six, pbr, mock, path.py, greenlet, enum-compat, eventlet, pyyaml, wrapt, werkzeug, amqp, anyjson, komb
u, urllib3, idna, chardet, certifi, requests, nameko
Successfully installed amqp-1.4.9 anyjson-0.3.3 certifi-2017.4.17 chardet-3.0.4 enum-compat-0.0.2 eventlet-0.21.0 greenlet-0.4.12 idn
a-2.5 kombu-3.0.37 mock-2.0.0 nameko-2.6.0 path.py-10.3.1 pbr-3.1.1 pyyaml-3.12 requests-2.18.1 six-1.10.0 urllib3-1.21.1 werkzeug-0.
12.2 wrapt-1.10.10
You are using pip version 8.1.1, however version 9.0.1 is available.
You should consider upgrading via the 'pip install --upgrade pip' command.
devesh@devesh-VirtualBox:~$
```

 Be aware though that nameko won't actually work until we install some other software as well. More on that is covered in the *Things to know before using nameko* section.

Running and connecting a microservice using nameko

Looking at the nameko version of our `person` service, it's clear that the effort paid off. Our service is defined by a class with the `name` attribute and several member functions decorated with RPC, as shown in the following code example:

```
from nameko.rpc import rpc

from .person import Person


class PersonAPI:
    name = 'person'

    @rpc
    def create(self, first_name, last_name, age, member = False):
        return Person.create(first_name, last_name, age, member).id

    @rpc
    def list(self):
        return [x.as_dict() for x in Person.list()]

    @rpc
    def get(self, id):
        return Person.load(id).as_dict()

    @rpc
    def set(self, id, **values):
        person = Person.load(id)

        for name, value in values.items():
            setattr(person, name, value)

        person.store()

    @rpc
    def delete(self, id):
        Person.load(id).delete()
```

The member functions interface with the same database interface class we used in the previous section. In a very straightforward way, it would even be reasonable to combine the two into one class, and that's it-the complete definition of our microservice using nameko. Pretty sweet, right? It really is, but every cloud has a silver lining, as we'll soon see.

Things to know before using nameko

Nameko is great, but there are things we need to be aware of before we choose nameko or any similar tool.

The first thing to be aware of is that nameko doesn't provide the complete AMQP infrastructure, it just connects to it.

> The AMQP infrastructure is responsible for conveying messages between connected programs in a way that is quick and reliable.

This means that we need an AMQP server running somewhere that nameko can find it and an AMQP server accessible to the microservice's users, and those servers need to be connected to each other.

They could be the same server, of course, but they don't have to be. Nameko recommends the RabbitMQ AMQP server, which can be downloaded from its own website (`www.rabbitmq.com`). The installation is relatively uncomplicated and there are detailed instructions on the site.

Interacting with our microservice

Now that we have an AMQP server installed and running, can we connect or service and manipulate person objects? Technically yes, but we need to use nameko to write the client too.

> AMQP isn't as simple to work with as HTTP, and the RPC mechanism adds an additional layer of complexity. We don't want to work with that raw.

There are two ways to interact with our microservice. Let's examine them in a bit more detail.

Interacting with a microservice manually using the nameko shell

The first way we can interact with our microservice is manually using the nameko shell, which is an enhanced Python shell. First, we have to run the microservice, which we'll do in its own command window, running the following command:

```
nameko run demo_nameko.service
```

Then, we'll start the `nameko` shell and use the end `RPC` object to access the functions of our microservice, as shown in the following code example:

```
(nameko) $ nameko shell --interface plain
Nameko Python 3.5.2 (default, Sep 28 2016, 13:06:15)
[GCC 4.9.3] shell on linux
Broker: b'amqp://guest:guest@localhost'
>>> n.rpc.person.create('Dave', 'Soiree', 48)
2
>>> n.rpc.person.delete(2)
>>> █
```

Here, it looks like we're just calling the functions, but actually we're communicating with the microservice through the AMQP protocol.

Interacting with a microservice by creating another microservice

The second way we can interact with our microservice is to create another microservice that depends on it, as shown in the following code example found in the `test.py` file:

```python
from nameko.rpc import RpcProxy
from nameko.timer import timer
from pprint import pprint


class TestService:
    name = 'test_person'

    person = RpcProxy('person')

    @timer(interval = 10)
    def test(self):
        pprint(self.person.list())

        candide = self.person.create('Candide', 'Apples', 25)
        pprint(candide)

        pprint(self.person.list())

        self.person.set(candide, age = 27)

        pprint(self.person.get(candide))

        self.person.delete(candide)

        pprint(self.person.list())
```

The `TestService` class periodically exercises the `person`service. It also demonstrates how to link one service to another, so that one of them is able to access the other. The key is this line, which creates an `RpcProxy` instance on the class:

```
person = RpcProxy('person')
```

When the service runs, it's able to access the functions of the specified remote service through that object. To run our tests, we need to start both the `person` microservice and the `test` microservice, which we can do with a single command, as shown in the following code:

```
nameko run demo_nameko.service demo_nameko.test
```

You may have noticed that we return the object `id` from the `create` function, rather than create a `person` object itself. That's because we can't return the `person` object.

Nameko functions can return any data that can be represented as JSON, but that doesn't include instances of arbitrary classes. The same goes for parameters that are passed into the functions of a microservice; they need to be within the limits of JSON.

This isn't actually a more stringent restriction than what we saw in the Flask microservice (in the previous section). It's just that with Flask it was obvious we were sending data across the network in JSON format, so that limitation was obvious. With nameko, the requirement is the same, but the reason for it is easier to miss.

Summary

At the start of the chapter, we looked at what microservices are philosophically and what their advantages are, and implemented an HTTP-oriented microservice using Flask.

We then looked at some of the advantages of process-based modularity and saw how applying those principles to web applications results in a microservice architecture. We looked at the details needed to use Flask to create a RESTful microservice and put that knowledge to use by building a simple person management microservice.

Next, we looked at using nameko's RPC mechanism to implement a microservice, which simplifies the code significantly, at the cost of requiring that we set up an AMQP infrastructure and a more difficult interface with systems outside the AMQP network.

In the next chapter, we'll look at how to interface between Python and compiled code to optimize performance bottlenecks in our code and access libraries written in other programming languages.

12
Extension Modules and Compiled Code

In this chapter, we'll discuss how to integrate compiled code into Python programs. We'll take a look at the benefits and drawbacks of our compiled code and see two ways of making a connection between Python's managed environment and code that runs directly on the hardware.

We'll see how to use the `ctypes` package and tie it to the interface of a C dynamic library, calling its functions and receiving their output from within our Python code. We'll also look at an easy way to write compiled code modules so that they could be imported and called directly from Python.

We'll cover the following topics in detail:

- Advantages and disadvantages of compiled code
- Accessing a dynamic library using `ctypes`
- Interfacing with C code using Cython

Advantages and disadvantages of compiled code

There are many real advantages of using compiled code. Python is a very productive language, but it may not fulfil the requirements of a lot of people. Sometimes, we need to interface with code written in a different language. One reason for doing this would be in case we need to access some functionality that is written in a different language that doesn't exist in Python.

As long as the code in question is in a dynamic library that has a C-compatible interface, it's relatively easy to call the code from within Python, using the **Foreign Function Interface (FFI)** provided by Python's standard ctypes package, which we'll discuss in the next section.

Alternatively, we may need to write some code that runs **Close to Metal (CTM)**, either to maximize the performance of an algorithm that's proven to be a bottleneck in our project, or interface directly with some piece of hardware. In this case, we'll need to compile custom code and link it to the Python environment. You can easily do this using a tool called **Cython** (for more details, refer to cython.org), which we'll discuss in the third section of this chapter.

The downsides of compiled code

While working with compiled code is usually absolutely fine, there can be some significant downsides. Let's take a look at them:

- First and foremost is the fact that it's easy to create ridiculously weird bugs when we work at this level of compiled code. Both `ctypes` and Cython allow us to make a horrible mess in the program's memory, potentially producing any conceivable kind of bug or error. The following diagram illustrates an example of a potential low-level bug. You can imagine how difficult it would be to troubleshoot such bugs.

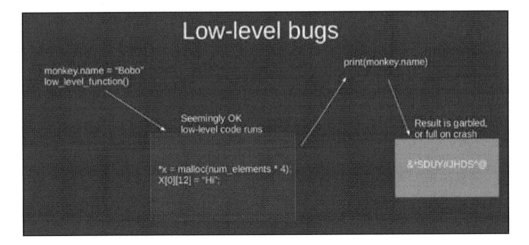

If we're lucky, that bug or error would result in a flat-out termination of our program, that is, if it violates the constraints of the operating system's protected memory manager.

I say we'll be lucky because if that doesn't happen, it would mean we've made an effective random change to some part of our program state and who knows what that'll do.

- The second downside is that it makes distributing our program more difficult. For a normal Python program, we can distribute a single .pyz file to our users or upload a set of tools, a compatible source package, or a neutral operating system wheel file to the **Python Package Index (PyPI)**. Using compiled code means we have to worry about which operating system and hardware architecture our users employ and provide separate packages for each combination we want to support.

- The third downside only applies if we're writing our own compiled code primarily for those use cases where Cython is most useful. The problem is that it could be complex to actually get a compiler installed and working, particularly for people who aren't used to working with compilers. Not only that, if we distribute our project as source code, our users would need to go through the same hassle.

Between the danger of bizarre errors and the annoyance involved in creating and distributing projects that use compiled code, we should generally wait until we have a compelling reason for taking the step of creating or interfacing with compiled code.

Now we have a pretty good grasp of the benefits of interfacing with compiled code: it gives us access to C-compatible libraries written in other languages. This code lets us optimize the performance of critical algorithms, and it lets us interface directly with hardware or low-level drivers.

Similarly, we know what the drawbacks are, namely the potential and seemingly inexplicable errors and a generally higher level of annoyance and difficulty throughout the development and distribution process. Now, let's take a look at putting some of the knowledge we've gained into action.

Accessing a dynamic library using ctypes

In this section, we're going to narrow down our focus to the Python standard library's ctypes package, which allows us to interact with dynamic libraries from within Python.

Locating and linking a dynamic library

Probably, the most common need to interact with compiled code is when there's a library out there that does exactly what we need but it's not a Python library. Perhaps it was instead written for C, or it has a C interface.

We're not going to let a little thing like this stop us. Instead, we'll use ctypes to create an interface module for the library. For basic usage, ctypes is very simple. We just need to import it, load the dynamic library by the filename, and call a function in that library as shown in the following code example:

```
>>> import ctypes
>>> libc = ctypes.CDLL('libc.so.6')
>>> libc.printf('Hello, foreign function interface!\n')
1
H>>>
```

The CDLL constructor we called in this example creates a Python object that represents a dynamic library containing C functions. We do need to take care when we define the filename of the library here, because of course different operating systems have different naming conventions for their libraries. The libc.so.6 attribute, in our example here, is the filename of the C standard library on current versions of Linux.

The `ctypes` package includes a utility function, called `ctypes.util.find_library`, to help address this difficulty. If we pass a base name to `find_library`, it will try to find the full name of the version installed on the system, as shown in the following code example:

```
>>> import ctypes.util
>>> ctypes.util.find_library('c')
'libc.so.6'
>>>
```

The `ctypes.util.find_library` is pretty useful on Linux and Mac OS X but less so on Windows because Windows dynamic libraries handle multiple versions in a very different way.
It's also worth noting that when we pass the C string to `find_library`, we'll find the C standard library on Linux and Mac OS X. On Windows, the same library is rather arbitrarily called `msvcrt`.

For cross-platform library loading, we need to be able to specify several alternate names for the library; try `find_library` on these names (refer to the following code example) and fall back to trying the raw name if `find_library` fails.

```
def load_library(*alternates):
    for base_name in alternates:
        lib_name = ctypes.util.find_library(base_name)

        try:
            if lib_name:
                return ctypes.CDLL(lib_name)
            else:
                return ctypes.CDLL(base_name)
        except OSError:
            pass

    raise OSError ('Unable to load any of: {}'.format(alternates))
```

There's a `load_library` function in the `demo_ctype/libc.py` file, available with this book, which also demonstrates this.

Accessing functions defined in the library

Once we have the library loaded, we have access to the functions exported from that library, which are exposed as attributes of the library object in Python. We saw this in the previous section when we called C's `printf` function.

Now, it's important to know that there's nothing in the C shared library that tells the users of the library what the parameter types of a function are, or the return type, or even how many parameters the function has. This information is used when compiling the library, but it isn't part of the end result. This means it's up to us to know how the function is supposed to be used. For example, the C library contains a quick sort function called `qsort`, which is intended to accept several parameters. Let's see what happens if these parameters aren't provided:

```
>>> libc.qsort()
Segmentation fault (core dumped)
bhagya@bhagya-VirtualBox:~$
```

As you can see in the preceding code example, if we omit the parameters, `ctypes` has no way of knowing whether we're making a mistake, and bad things happen with no warning.

Assigning attributes to a function

If we're planning on making systematic use of a foreign function, or especially, if we're going to expose it as part of the interface of a module we're writing, it is advisable to tell `ctypes` about the function's signature. We can do this by assigning to the function's `argtypes` and `restype` attributes.

The `argtypes` attribute should be a list of C data types defined in the `ctypes` package, while `restype` should be one of these packages, as shown in the following code example:

```
>>> libc.atof.argtypes = [ctypes.c_char_p]
>>> libc.atof.restype = ctypes.c_double
>>> libc.atof('12.3')
Traceback (most recent call last):
  File "<stdin>", line 1, in <module>
ctypes.ArgumentError: argument 1: <class 'TypeError'>: wrong type
>>> libc.atof("12.3")
Traceback (most recent call last):
  File "<stdin>", line 1, in <module>
ctypes.ArgumentError: argument 1: <class 'TypeError'>: wrong type
>>> ctypes.atof()
Traceback (most recent call last):
  File "<stdin>", line 1, in <module>
AttributeError: module 'ctypes' has no attribute 'atof'
>>> libc.atof()
Traceback (most recent call last):
  File "<stdin>", line 1, in <module>
TypeError: this function takes at least 1 argument (0 given)
>>>
```

As you can see in the code, providing this information to `ctypes` significantly improves the error handling of a foreign function. The `atof` function returns a double-precision floating point number, but `ctypes` wouldn't know about this if we don't tell it so. When `ctypes` doesn't have the information, it just assumes the return value is an integer; this works in many cases, but it would have been useless in this particular example.

Using a pointer as a parameter of a function

It's pretty common for C functions to accept a pointer as one of the parameters and fill in a value at the address that the pointer refers to. Naturally, `ctypes` allows us to work with this sort of interface by letting us create objects that represent memory locations and passing that object using the pointer to the functions we call. The C `scanf` function works in a way that can be illustrated by the following code example:

```
>>> integer = ctypes.c_int()
>>> decimal = ctypes.c_float()
>>> libc.scanf(b'%i %f', ctypes.byref(integer), ctypes.byref(decimal))
5 3.14
2
>>> integer
c_int(5)
>>> decimal
c_float(3.140000104904175)
>>>
```

In this example, we created two C-style variables called `integer` and `decimal`; then, we used the `scanf` function to fill them with values, based on user input. The `byref` function tells `ctypes` that we're not passing the value of the variable to the function, but that we're passing its memory address, so the function can store something there.

Providing a function signature

Another common behavior of C functions is filling bytes into a character buffer. We can use the `create_string_buffer` function of `ctypes` to allocate such a buffer and then use the result as a parameter for functions that want a string buffer, as shown in the following code example:

```
from .libc import printf, scanf, localtime, asctime
from ctypes import c_int, create_string_buffer, byref, Structure

def input_pair():
    key = c_int()
    value = create_string_buffer(16)
    printf(b"[Input a pair as int:string] ")
    scanf(b"%i:%s", byref(key), byref(value))
    return key, value.value

def print_a_time():
    timer = c_int(12345678)
    printf(asctime(localtime(byref(timer))))
```

Let's look at this code now. We do not need to use the `byref` function here, because the character bumper is inherently by reference. There's just no other way to do this in C.

There's a pitfall here: one that's been tripping up C programmers for decades. Our string buffer has a specific length, but the function we're passing to it doesn't know what that length is. If it starts writing to the buffer and continues beyond the end of the buffer, the program will either crash or begin behaving strangely. Always make sure your buffer is at least large enough for whatever will be written into it.

Providing data structure layouts

Another thing that is not available in a C shared library is the layout of data structures that the functions use, as shown in the following code example:

```
struct tm
{
  int tm_sec;                   /* Seconds.   [0-60] (1 leap second) */
  int tm_min;                   /* Minutes.   [0-59] */
  int tm_hour;                  /* Hours.     [0-23] */
  int tm_mday;                  /* Day.       [1-31] */
  int tm_mon;                   /* Month.     [0-11] */
  int tm_year;                  /* Year -   1900.   */
  int tm_wday;                  /* Day of week. [0-6] */
  int tm_yday;                  /* Days in year. [0-365] */
  int tm_isdst;                 /* DST.       [-1/0/1]*/

#ifdef___USE_MISC
  long int tm_gtoff;            /* Seconds east of UTC.   */
  const char *tm_zone;          /* Timezone abbreviation.  */
#else
  long int__tn_gtoff;           /* Seconds east of UTC.   */
  const char *__tm_zone;        /* Timezone abbreviation.  */
#endif
};
```

Again, `ctypes` gives us a way of filling in the missing information. C's `tm` structure, which is used for representing date and time information, looks like the following code:

```
_libc = load_library('c', 'msvcrt')

class tm(ctypes.Structure):
    _fields_ = [
        ('tm_sec', ctypes.c_int),
        ('tm_min', ctypes.c_int),
        ('tm_hour', ctypes.c_int),
        ('tm_mday', ctypes.c_int),
        ('tm_mon', ctypes.c_int),
        ('tm_year', ctypes.c_int),
        ('tm_wday', ctypes.c_int),
        ('tm_yday', ctypes.c_int),
        ('tm_isdst', ctypes.c_int),
    ]

printf = _libc.printf

scanf = _libc.scanf

localtime = _libc.localtime
localtime.argtypes = [ctypes.POINTER(ctypes.c_int)]
localtime.restype = ctypes.POINTER(tm)

asctime = _libc.asctime
asctime.argtypes = [ctypes.POINTER(tm)]
asctime.restype = ctypes.c_char_p
```

As shown in this example, the translation into ctypes is straightforward. We need to create a class that would inherit from ctypes.Structure, and in that class, we need to create a list called **fields** containing tuples of field name and field type.

Once we get this, we could create instances of the class and assign the attributes as we'd expect in Python. But, we can also pass it to C functions as a parameter, either directly or by reference, and we can use it as part of the signature of a foreign function.

The ctypes package provides support for pretty much every feature of the C language, but we've now seen the ones that are most useful for calling into a library function and using its results.

Interfacing with C code using Cython

In this section, we're going to look at a third-party tool called Cython, which is another tool for bridging the gap between Python and the software that has been compiled into machine code.

If we have a situation where we want to implement part of our project in compiled code, we could do this by creating a dynamic library containing the code and calling to it with ctypes; however, that's a roundabout way to get where we want to go. We'd end up writing a lot of code twice: once for the sake of our compiler and then again to tell ctypes about details such as function signatures and data structures.

Now this is inefficient and violates one of the most important principles of programming—*don't repeat yourself*. There's a tool that's better suited to this situation, as you may have surely guessed, and that tool is Cython.

Working with Cython

What Cython does is it translates a Python source code file into a C source code file containing equivalent calls to the Python C API; then it wraps it in the boilerplate necessary to turn it into a Python binary module.

This would be useful enough by itself, but Cython also allows us to inject calls in C functions and low-level data access operations into the module. The end result is that we could pretty much just write our compiled code as if it were Python and still gain the speed or low-level access that prompted our need to compile it in the first place.

The amount of work this saves us over using the Python API directly is considerable. The 100-line Python example included with this course translates into more than 5,000 lines of C when compiled. Let's go through this example piece by piece and talk about the differences while comparing it with plain Python.

Additional import methods in Cython

Cython allows two import mechanisms in addition to the normal ones provided by Python packages. Let's check out these mechanisms in detail.

The first mechanism is called `cimport`, and it imports the signatures of compiled functions and data structures from pre-prepared libraries, as shown in the following command line:

```
from cpython.mem cimport PyMem_Malloc, PyMem_Realloc, PyMem_Free
```

In this case, since Cython comes with a pre-prepared library of all Python C API functions, we were able to use this mechanism to report the needed information about Python's low-level memory allocation and de-allocation functions.

The second additional importing mechanism is `cdef extern from`. When we don't already have the signature of a compiled function available, we use the syntax to make it available in the Cython code.

The indented block can contain any number of function declarations, type definitions, structure definitions, and so on, as shown in the following code example. Note that these don't need to be precisely correct, though, just close enough that Cython is able to generate proper C code:

```
cdef extern from "string.h":
    void *memcpy(void *str1, const void *str2, size_t n)
```

A `cdef extern from` block references a C header file, which is automatically included in the generated C code. While we could simply use the normal Python syntax for the `class` statement, prepending it with `cdef` gives the ability to store raw data values in predefined variable members of the class instances, as shown in the following code example:

```
cdef class StatisticalArray:
    cdef double* values
    cdef int num_values
    cdef int max_values
```

Writing extension modules in Cython

The `num_values` variable in the previous code example is just a chunk of memory that stores bits that represent an integer value. It doesn't have any of the extra data needed to turn it into a Python object.

 This is a bad thing in a way because it means that Python can't do any of the smart things it does to help us write good code quickly. We wouldn't be working with these tools if we didn't have a reason to let them do some of this work for us.

So, to resolve this, let's define an extension type called `StatisticalArray` (refer to the following code example), which contains a pointer to a memory location and two integers. The memory location is supposed to contain double-precision floating point numbers. These are raw machine-level values, and while primitive in comparison to Python values, they're very fast because they can be fed directly into CPU operations.

```
def __cinit__(StatisticalArray self, StatisticalArray copy_from = None, *pargs, **kwargs):
    if copy_from:
        self.num_values = copy_from.num_values
        self.max_values = copy_from.num_values
        self.values = <double*> PyMem_Malloc(copy_from.max_values * sizeof(double))
        memcpy(self.values, copy_from.values, copy_from.num_values * sizeof(double))
    else:
        self.values = NULL
        self.num_values = 0
        self.max_values = 0

def __dealloc__(StatisticalArray self):
    if self.values != NULL:
        PyMem_Free(self.values)
```

In this code example, we have the functions that set up and dispose of the instances of the `StatisticalArray` class.

Notice that the setup function is called `__cinit__`, not `__init__`. Actually, a Cython `cdef` class can have both. The `__cinit__` function's job is to set up the raw variables for the class instance, and the normal `__init__` function is supposed to set up any normal Python variable it contains.

The `__cinit__` function is called first, and it's not guaranteed that `self` will actually be a valid Python object itself yet, so it should confine itself only to initializing raw variables. The reason `__cinit__` accepts the extra positional and keyword arguments is because if a Python class inherits from our class and adds more parameters to the signature of `__init__`, the `__cinit__` function will still work.

At the other end of the process, we have the __dealloc__ function, which needs to release any specially allocated resources associated with the class instance. In the preceding case, we allocated a chunk of memory to __cinit__, so we need to release that memory in the __dealloc__ function.

Methods to increase the execution speed of Python code

Now we are going to define a few of Python's normal magic methods, which will allow us to iterate over the values stored in our object and access them by indexing. For this, refer to the following code example:

```
def __iter__(StatisticalArray self):
    cdef int index
    for index in range(self.num_values):
        yield self.values[index]

def __getitem__(StatisticalArray self, int index):
    if index < 0
        index = index + self.num_values

    if index < 0 or index >= self.num_values:
        raise IndexError(index)

    return self.values[index]

def __setitem__(StastisticalArray self, int index, double value):
    if index < 0
        index = index + self.num_values

    if index < 0 or index >= self.num_values:

    self.values[index] = value
```

The thing to notice in this code example is how little has changed from what we've be doing in a pure Python implementation. The only real differences are the type definitions we provided for every parameter and the local variable.

 We didn't actually have to provide the type definition for every parameter and local variable. The type definition lets Cython generate plain C code for a lot of the operations we're performing, which means we're using the CPU directly instead of the Python virtual machine. We're trading flexibility for speed.

The previous functions were all defined with the def keyword as normal for Python, and these functions operate as if they were defined in a normal Python module.

Cython gives us two other options, though. Instead of def, we can use cdef; in this case, the function is much faster to call, but it's only for use by other Cython code. This is great for internal help functions and such. Alternatively, we can use cpdef (as shown in the following code example); here, the function is accessible from normal Python, but it's almost as fast as a cdef function when called from Cython code:

```
cpdef append(StatisticalArray self, double value)
    if self.num_values == self.max_values:
        self.max_values = self.max_values * 2 if self.max_values > 0 else 8
        self.values = <double*> PyMem_Realloc(self.values,  self.max_values * sizeof(double))

    self.values[self.num_values] = value

    self.num_value += 1
```

We've chosen cpdef in our case because we want to expose the full feature set to any Python code that uses our compiled module, but we also expect to use the same functionality from within our Cython code.

Using cpdef in a Cython class

In the following code example, you'll see that we're getting to the reason why we called our class `StatisticalArray`. We implemented several discrete statistical calculations using the values stored in the class instance. You don't need to worry about what `mean`, `variance`, and `covariance` actually do, but let's take a look at how they're actually working.

```
cpdef double mean(StatisticalArray self):
    cdef int index
    cdef double total = 0.0

    for index in range(self.num_values):
        total += self.values[index]

    return total / self.num_values

cpdef double variance(StatisticalArray self)
    cdef statisticalArray temp = StatisticalArray()
    cdef double mean = self.mean()
    cdef int index

    for index in range(self.num_values):
        temp.append((self.values[index] - mean) ** 2)

    return temp.mean()

cpdef double covariance(StatisticalArray self, StatisticalArray other) except? -200.0:
    if self.num_values != other.num_values:
        raise ValueError("Array sizes differ")

    cdef SatisticalArray temp = StatisticalArray()
    cdef double self_mean = self.mean()
    cdef double other_mean = self.mean()
    cdef int index

    for index in range(self.num_values):
        temp.append((self.values[index] - self_mean) * (other.values[index] - other_mean))
```

In the `mean` function, here, we see a loop that calculates the sum of the values stored in the array. If we were running that code in Python, each cycle through the loop would involve several dictionary lookups and function calls. Cython generates four lines of C code for this that translates into only a few machine code operations.

This is possible because we told Cython that the `index` variable should be a C integer, and because Cython is smart about handling loops with C integer variables, we gain a similar benefit in both `variance` and `covariance` functions. Again, we just use the Python syntax and give Cython additional information that it can use to optimize the generated code.

There is one unusual thing to note with `covariance`, though. At the end of the first line shown in the following screenshot, we see `except? -200.0`:

```
cpdef double covariance(StatisticalArray self, Statistical other) except?
-200.0
```

What is that? Well, as with most of these functions, we gave the `covariance` function an explicit C return type of `double`. That's a big gain in terms of speed. But when the code calling the function is also Cython, and stores the return value in a `cdef` double variable, there's a downside. Normally, Cython would use the return value to signal that an exception has been raised, but how is it supposed to do that when we have changed the return type, since it cannot know which values are valid at that point?

Well, we'll tell it. Adding `except? -200.0` means that if the return value is −200, Cython would check to see whether an exception has been raised. If we had left off `?`, it would have meant that −200 always means there's an exception, which is a bit faster; however, we can't go that far because −200 is still a potentially valid return variable.

Notice that we don't actually return −200; we just raise an exception as normal. Cython takes care of the rest. Here are a couple of more examples of functions that are built using the earlier functions as building blocks:

```
cpdef double standard_deviation(StasticalArray self):
    return self.variance() ** 0.5

cpdef double pearson_coefficient(StasticalArray self, StasticalArray other) except? -200.0:
    return self.covariance(other) / (self.standard_deviation() * other.standard_deviation())
```

Thanks to our use of `cpdef`, when we define the `variance` and `covariance` functions, there's very little overhead involved in calling those functions from here.

Compiling an extension module in Python

So let's say we've written a somewhat useful Cython class; now, how do we make it available to Python code? Well, we have to compile it.

First of all, this means we need to have a compiler. The documentation on cython.org has a tutorial entry and appendix on this process, and I suggest you refer to them if there's not already a compiler on your system. If you have a compiler, installing Cython is just a matter of asking `pip` to grab it for us:

```
python3.5 -m pip install Cython
```

The installation can be a little slow because it needs to do some compiling during the installation; just be patient until it finishes.

Once Cython is installed, we need to create a `setup.py` file describing how to build our extension, as shown in the following code example. For the base case, the process is very straightforward.

The source code we were working on is saved in `statistics.pyx`, as shown in the following code example. The `.pyx` extension is the standard filename extension for Cython source code files.

```
from distutils.core import setup
from Cython.Build import cythonize

setup(
    ext_modules = cythonize('statistics.pyx')
)
```

Once we do this, the last step is a snap. Once the `build_ext` command is finished, we should have a compiled extension sitting next to our `.pyx` file.

Now, all we have to do is import it and use it as follows:

```
>>> import statistics
>>> import random
>>> a = statistics.StatisticalArray()
>>> a,append(random.random())
Traceback (most recent call last):
  File "<stdin>", line 1, in <module>
NameError: name 'append' is not defined
>>> a.append(random.random())
>>> a.append(random.random())
>>> a.append(random.random())
>>> a.append(random.random())
>>> b = statistics.StatisticalArray()
>>> b.append(random.random())
>>> b.append(random.random())
>>> b.append(random.random())
>>> a.pearson_coefficient(b)
Traceback (most recent call last):
  File "<stdin>", line 1, in <module>
  File "statistics.pyx", line 94, in statistics.StatisticalArray.pearson_coefficient (statistics.c:2537)
    cpdef double pearson_coefficient(StatisticalArray self, StatisticalArray other) except? -200.0:
  File "statistics.pyx", line 95, in statistics.StatisticalArray.pearson_coefficient (statistics.c:2476)
    return self.covariance(other) / (self.standard_deviation() * other.standard_deviation())
  File "statistics.pyx", line 79, in statistics.StatisticalArray.covariance (statistics.c:2135)
    raise ValueError("Array sizes differ")
ValueError: Array sizes differ
>>> ▮
```

Notice that when we cause an exception in the compiled code, the traceback is fully filled in and points us to the cause and location of the problem. That's a Cython feature and a nice advantage.

Summary

In this chapter, we discussed the benefits and drawbacks of using compiled code. We took a look at using Python's standard `ctypes` package to access functions stored in compiled C-compatible dynamic libraries, which is a quick way to gain access to the functionality that was written in other languages.

We also saw how to use Cython to operate with one foot at Python's higher level and C's much lower level of abstraction, with surprisingly little pain involved in bridging the gap. We can use this knowledge to optimize bottlenecks in our programs or access functionality that's only available when we operate close to the hardware.

With this, we've come to the end of this course. I hope you've learned a lot and have gained immense knowledge about Python. Keep learning!

Index

Printed in Great Britain
by Amazon